The English Essay

Writing about literature

Hugh Robertson

The English Essay
Writing about Literature

Second Edition

Copyright © 1993, 2000. Piperhill Publications.
All rights reserved.

ISBN 0-9693068-5-7

Printed and bound in Canada

Canadian Cataloguing in Publication Data

Robertson, Hugh, 1939—
The English essay: writing about literature

2nd ed.
Includes bibliographical references
ISBN 0-9693068-5-7

1. Report writing. 2. Exposition (Rhetoric)   I. Title

LB2369.R63 1998   808'.02   C98-901043-0

Cover Design: Richard N. Strong, R.G.D., MGDC, Ottawa
Interior Design: Avante Graphics, Sharper Images

This book was manufactured in Canada using acid-free and recycled paper.

CONTENTS

ACKNOWLEDGEMENTS

The English Essay has undergone a major transformation and expansion since it was first published in 1993. I would like to express my appreciation to the following people who, through their expertise, erudition, and experience, have helped to shape the transformation: Tony Horava, Dr. Wayne Howell, Professor Robert MacDonald, Kel Morin-Parsons, and Margo Whittaker.

In particular, I would like to pay special tribute to the supportive role played by Hugh Penton. His perceptive comments and practical suggestions, based on extensive experience as a dedicated teacher, have proved invaluable in the preparation of the new edition.

The following students kindly provided sample assignments to illustrate the writing techniques described in *The English Essay*: Rick Bowness, Richard Holliday, Alison Howell, David Maxwell, Jennifer Polk, Brian Quan, and Kerry Roulston. I am grateful for their thoughtful contributions.

For my wife and sons

Introduction

An essay is not a creative writing assignment, nor is it an exposition of factual information. It is neither a personal narrative, a biographical chronicle, nor a descriptive composition. **An essay has an argument, or point of view, or thesis.** It is your point of view imprinted on an essay or term paper that distinguishes it from other types of writing — no argument, no essay.[1] *The English Essay* takes you step by step through the process of writing various types of essays on literary genres such as plays, poems, short stories, and novels. It can be used for writing about works of literature in any modern language.

The process described in this manual is the result of many years of teaching students of various ages. It is a practical process that has been thoroughly tried and tested. It is not a rigid formula but a flexible model that you can adapt to suit your own individual needs, whether you prefer to use the latest computer technology or a more traditional approach. While topics from various works of literature are used to demonstrate the process, the method can be used for essays and term papers in most of the humanities. The method can also be modified for descriptive and narrative assignments, reports, book reviews, examinations, and oral presentations, such as seminars.

The manual launches the process of writing an essay on a literary topic by focusing on a single primary text, and then advances step by step through increasingly more complex assignments. Since the stages are built one upon the other, it is important that you read the sections in the order in which they appear, to understand the process.

The academic essay is the basis of much professional writing: legal briefs, business reports, arts reviews, newspaper editorials, and scholarly articles are all variations on the theme of the academic essay. Essay writing develops many skills: organization skills, communication skills, thinking skills, and time-management skills. It also promotes and fosters qualities such as insight, imagination, and initiative. These talents are useful not only in school and university; they are life-skills of great relevance and wide application.

There is no "last word" on any literary text, there is no definitive interpretation by a literary luminary — all readers who bring their intellects and emotions to bear on a work of literary art are capable of providing unique insights and responses. Art scholars have been studying Michelangelo's Sistine Chapel paintings for over four hundred years, but it was only a few years ago that a tourist pointed out something that had eluded everyone else: in the "Creation of Adam" scene — the famous one in which God extends his arm and gives the spark of life to Adam's outstretched finger — the composition of the figures around the deity represents, with quite remarkable accuracy, the shape of the human brain. If you look carefully at a literary text through the prism of your own life and experience, you might be surprised at what you can discover.

Every essay is, to some extent, a journey of exploration and discovery into unknown intellectual and emotional territory. We offer a pathway to guide you as you embark on your exciting and challenging quest.

THE PRIMARY TEXT ESSAY

Introduction

There is neither a shortage of types of writing assignments in literature courses, nor a shortage of terms used by instructors to describe the various types of assignments. The terminology can be confusing. Some terms such as "discuss" are vague, while others like "analyze" have a variety of interpretations and applications. What is the difference between "exposition" and "argumentation"? What is an "interpretive essay" or a "critical essay"?

Unfortunately, there is no agreement — not even among instructors — as to the precise meaning of these terms. Thus it is essential that you consult your instructors individually to discuss and define terminology before beginning your assignments. Develop a glossary so that you have a clear understanding of the terms that you are using. **Precise use of terminology is crucial to successful assignments.**

Initially, your writing assignments will probably be based on a single primary text, such as a novel or a play. In this situation the instructor is interested in your reflections and responses to the text and not on the critical comments of literary scholars. It is important to develop your own skills of literary analysis before relying on secondary critical sources, lest you become dependent on the thinking of others. A primary text assignment will require you to read and interpret a literary work and your efforts should culminate in a well-structured and coherent response that explains in some way how the form of the work contributes to its meaning. This will entail listing the various literary techniques or devices that shape the work and then explaining how the most important ones serve to reveal the work's major themes or meaning.

3

Preparing the Essay

Let us assume that you are studying the modern short story in your literature course and your instructor has assigned "Boys and Girls" by Alice Munro as the topic for a short essay of 800–1000 words. You are also required to establish the focus for your essay. One of the major difficulties in essay writing is narrowing a broad topic to a specific focus. The failure to do so frequently results in a vague, superficial essay, lacking depth, detail, and direction. **Fixing your focus on a specific and significant aspect of the primary text is a crucial stage in preparing your essay.**

As a topic for an essay, "Boys and Girls" is too broad, so its scope must be narrowed. Your first task is to read the text and to prepare a list of aspects and features that could serve as a challenging focus for an analysis of the text. Imagine that your topic is a scene that you are viewing through a wide-angle zoom lens. You take note of all the important features in the field of vision and then you zoom in closer until a specific feature is clearly framed and focused. All your attention will now be concentrated on this feature. You can always zoom out again to check perspective and context if necessary.[2]

You can assemble a group of fellow students to brainstorm and exchange ideas on how to narrow the topic. As you read, think, discuss, and brainstorm, try to identify the major themes in the story, as well as the literary devices employed to reveal those themes. Thoughtful literary analysis hinges on discovering and then explaining the relationship between **content** — what is written, such as the themes — and **form** — how it is written, such as the use of literary devices. Jot these ideas down in a writing folder or a notebook or on a computer. It is a useful practice to keep a writing log or an *Ideas and Questions Journal* — an *"I.Q. Journal"* — in which to record your findings. For example, two separate lists of themes and literary devices drawn from "Boys and Girls" might include the possibilities shown on the opposite page. Alternatively, you could use a variety of diagrammatic techniques to list possible themes and devices.

Themes

- Role of women
- Role of men
- Role of children
- Stereotypes
- Love
- Loyalty
- Self-discovery
- Death
- Imprisonment and escape
- Isolation and alienation
- Cruelty

Devices

- Character development
- Use of dialogue
- Narrative point of view
- Plot structure
- Mood and atmosphere
- Setting
- Symbolism
- Metaphor and simile
- Conflict
- Tone
- Imagery
- Irony

Compose a short-list of themes to assist you in deciding on a focus for the essay. Then select one from your short-list on which to focus the essay. It is also a good idea to have one or two back-up ideas listed in your *I.Q. Journal* in case you run into difficulties with your first choice. Let us assume that, after careful consideration, you selected the theme of "self-discovery" as the focus for your essay on "Boys and Girls."

Since this theme reflects an aspect of the story's content, it is now necessary for you to select one or more literary devices from your list on page 5 so that you can set about the task of examining **how** the theme of self-discovery is explored. After considering your list of possibilities, you decide to examine how the major characters in the story are described and developed so as to shed light on the narrator's search for her identity. You have now established the focus of analysis for your essay. By isolating characterization as a device for exploring the theme of self-discovery, you have narrowed the focus even further — you have zoomed in closer. Do not forget to discuss your decision with the instructor to obtain approval before continuing.

Once you have narrowed your topic to a specific focus, you need to establish a clear sense of direction for the essay. **A concise and incisive question is the clearest means of giving direction and purpose to your essay.** Since the calibre of the question will influence the calibre of the essay, brainstorm potential questions and list them in your *I.Q. Journal.* Reflect on your list before deciding on your first choice, and then carefully fine-tune the phrasing so that it clearly spells out the purpose of the essay.

Since our interest is in the theme of self-discovery and the literary device of characterization, we might formulate the question as follows: How do the roles defined for the supporting characters in "Boys and Girls" serve to illustrate the narrator's search to discover her identity? The direction of the essay is clearly set out. Your task is to answer the question — that is the sole purpose of the assignment. **The answer will form your thesis, argument, or point of view.** Once again, check with your instructor to ensure that your question is acceptable and that it is appropriately phrased.

Since you have already read "Boys and Girls" to unlock interesting themes to explore, you will have a sound understanding of the story. You can now undertake a detailed analysis of the text in light of the question. Remember that your task is to develop a response to your question. Because you cannot remember everything you read, a systematic method for recording ideas, information, and examples is essential. **It is impossible to develop a good essay without an organized collection of notes.**

There are three ways in which you can record your notes. You can use index cards, standard notepaper, or a computer. We will use the notepaper method to illustrate the recording process for our essay on "Boys and Girls." Set up your notepaper recording system by ruling a right-hand margin of 2–3 cm on the front side of the page only, as shown below. Prepare a number of pages in advance so that you have a supply of notepaper for your notes.

As you reread the text, you will be looking specifically for ideas and examples pertaining to your question. On page 351 you notice a reference to Henry Bailey that emphasizes his roughhewn, uncouth character. Since this point is relevant to your question, you record it in the centre column of your notepaper as shown in the diagram below. You must identify the precise source of the note in case you need to cite it or refer to it for further details. Simply insert the page reference in the left-hand margin to identify the source of the note.

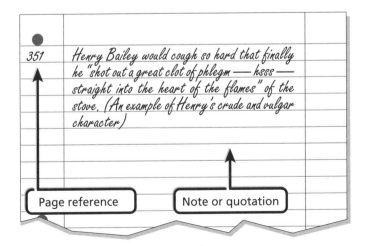

351   Henry Bailey would cough so hard that finally he "shot out a great clot of phlegm — hsss — straight into the heart of the flames" of the stove. (An example of Henry's crude and vulgar character)

Page reference   Note or quotation

Continue reading through the text, searching for ideas, information, and examples relevant to the question, and then record your insights and responses as just explained. On page 352 there is mention of how the girl imagines a world in which she is independent and powerful, and you decide to record the point verbatim in case you need a direct quotation to support your thesis. Copy the information accurately and use quotation marks to indicate that it is a quotation, as demonstrated below. The page reference is indicated in the left-hand margin. Nothing is written in the right-hand margin at this stage. Leave a line between each note so that the notes can be separated later. If you wish to make a comment about a quoted note, simply insert the comment in parentheses as shown below.

351	Henry Bailey would cough so hard that finally he "shot out a great clot of phlegm — hsss — straight into the heart of the flames" of the stove. (An example of Henry's crude and vulgar character)
352	"These stories were about myself, when I had grown a little older; they took place in a world that was recognizably mine, yet one that presented opportunities for courage, boldness, and self-sacrifice, as mine never did." (Imagines a world in which she is independent and powerful)

In recording the two notes above, you have:

• Discovered relevant examples pertaining to the question.

• Recorded them in note form.

• Indicated the page references.

The whole process of recording the ideas, information, and examples needed to develop your thesis is encapsulated in these three elements above. But the process is underpinned by continuous probing and questioning and by constant dissection and examination of your material.

Work through the text, questioning, analyzing, selecting, and recording the relevant information. A superficial reading will produce a superficial essay, but a passionate and thoughtful interaction with the text accompanied by perceptive questioning can generate original and creative ideas and responses. Do not record details just because they are "interesting." **Does the information help answer the question?** That must always be your criterion.

Once you have filled your first page of notepaper, continue on another page. Do not write on the reverse side of the page because it will be impossible to separate individual notes later during the outlining process.

The preparatory or pre-writing process — from narrowing the topic to formulating an incisive question to recording ideas, information, and examples — is an essential phase in building a quality essay. It is important that you set aside adequate time in your schedule for the preparatory work.

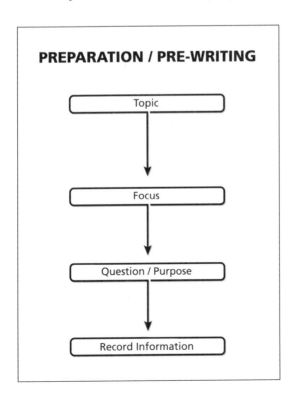

Writing the Essay

Once you have completed reading the text and recording your ideas and insights, you can start shaping and composing your answer to the question. Your answer or response represents **your argument, point of view, or thesis** — it is the axis on which the essay revolves.

Composing the answer is a crucial phase, because the success of your essay hinges on your ability to communicate your ideas clearly to the reader. Clarity of argument is largely dependent upon the style and the structure of your essay. Contrary to what many people think, structure does not suppress creativity; it promotes clear, creative expression.[3] The ABC formula below is a simple and effective model for structuring an essay. Style is the mortar that will hold it together.

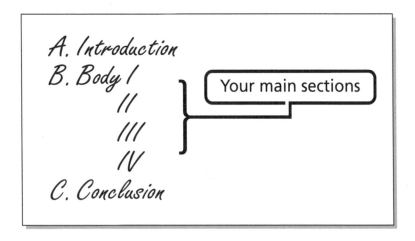

It is impossible to write the final copy straight from your notes. Shaping the structure of the essay is your initial task. The first step is to create an outline that imposes order on your notes and ideas. The method in this manual describes what might be called "conventional outlining." Some students might have alternative organizing systems, such as diagrammatic techniques. The nature of your system does not matter; **what is important is that you have an organizing system**.

Read through your notes, keeping the question uppermost in your mind. Try to isolate the main factors around which you can structure your essay. We have isolated five main factors in the body to illustrate how the roles of the supporting characters reveal the narrator's search for her identity. This list of main factors is called the **Basic Outline**, as shown below.

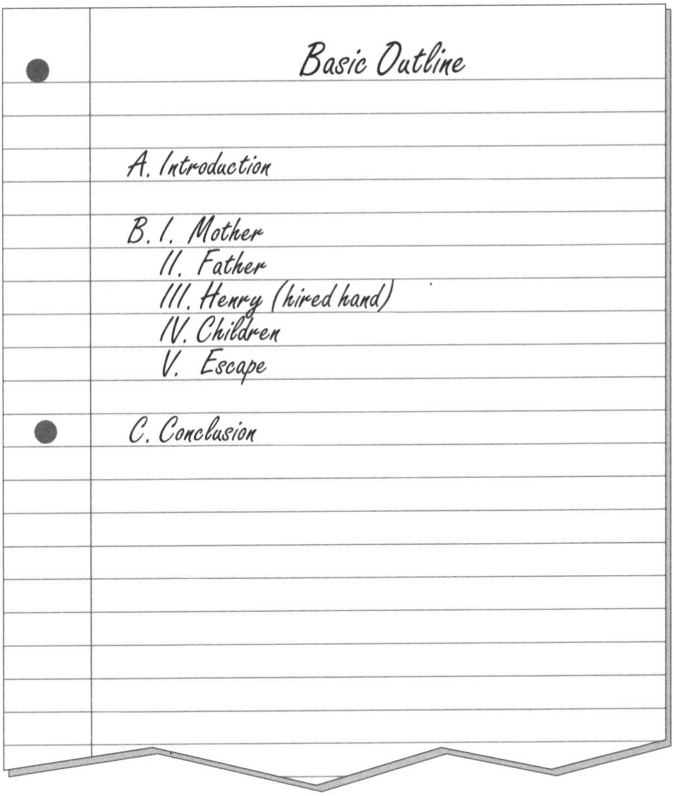

Basic Outline

A. Introduction

B. I. Mother
   II. Father
   III. Henry (hired hand)
   IV. Children
   V. Escape

C. Conclusion

Separate the individual notes with scissors — that is why you wrote on one side of the page only. Read through the separated notepaper slips and then group them according to the sections of the Basic Outline. The next step is to number the notepaper strips according to the sections of the Basic Outline into which they fall. Use the empty right-hand column to indicate the numbered section of the Basic Outline as shown below. For instance, all notes dealing with the role of the mother in the story are labeled "I" because "Mother" is section I of the Basic Outline, as shown on the previous page. It is a good idea to use paper clips to group the notepaper strips.

| 355 | Later the narrator comments that "it did not occur to me that she [her mother] could be lonely." | I |

Some notes will not fit into the major sections of the body or the introduction and they will have to be discarded. Do not be concerned if you cannot use all your notes. The rejected notes are not wasted: they are part of the "invisible foundations" that support your essay.

There is no magic number of body sections in a Basic Outline — from three to six will handle most questions. But **ensure that all sections address the question.** The basic structure of the essay is now in place, although it is possible that the actual order of the body sections may change later during the drafting stage.

The purpose of an essay is to develop an answer to the question and to articulate it in the form of an argument or thesis. In our example, we are not simply describing the characters in "Boys and Girls" or retelling the story — we are explaining the way in which we think the roles of the supporting characters reveal the narrator's search for her identity. Remember that when you are writing essays, **it is your point of view that is clearly stamped on each essay.**

For your point of view to be convincing, however, it needs substantial support. Once you have mapped out the overall structure in the Basic Outline, you need to isolate the supporting details for your argument. Take one section of your notes at a time and spread the notestrips on a table. Read through the notes carefully, selecting only what is essential to your argument. Ask yourself whether every idea, example, or quotation is directly relevant to the point of view you are developing.

The supporting details are arranged under the overall structure of the Basic Outline as shown below. This stage is known as the **Skeleton Outline.**

Skeleton Outline

A. Introduction

B. I. Mother
  - tragic heroine
  - isolation and dependence
  - longing for past/escape

II. Father
  - cold
  - stereotypical
  - contrast with mother

III. Henry (hired hand)
  - violent, e.g. horse
  - damaging to psyche of children
  - value of work

IV. Children
  - lack of regard for them
  - used as cheap labour

V. Escape
  - stories and singing
  - horse
  - return to reality

C. Conclusion

Allow time in your schedule to **rough out the complete essay** in a preliminary draft. With a detailed Skeleton Outline in place, preparing a rough draft will be quick and easy. One of the advantages of the outlines is that they provide a formula for developing your paragraphs. Remember that the clarity of your answer is your prime objective and that clarity is largely determined by the structure of your argument and the style of your expression. Paragraphs reflect the structure. In a short essay of less than a thousand words, the Basic Outline will provide the paragraph structure and the Skeleton Outline will supply the supporting details.

Skeleton Outline

A. Introduction   (Paragraph)

B. I. Mother   (Paragraph)
   -tragic heroine
   -isolation and dependence
   -longing for past/escape

   II. Father   (Paragraph)
   -cold
   -stereotypical
   -contrast with mother

   III. Henry (hired hand)   (Paragraph)
   -violent, e.g. horse
   -damaging to psyche of children
   -value of work

   IV. Children   (Paragraph)
   -lack of regard for them
   -used as cheap labour

   V. Escape   (Paragraph)
   -stories and singing
   -horse
   -return to reality

C. Conclusion   (Paragraph)

You will notice that the sample essay on pages 17–19 follows closely the overall ABC structure (introduction, body, conclusion) as well as the paragraph organization outlined on the previous page. In shorter essays on works of literature, where normally only one paragraph is required for the introduction, it is both difficult and awkward to integrate a question into the text of the introduction. **The key feature of the introduction is to state your response to the question** by conveying to the readers the line of argument you will pursue. This is commonly known as the **thesis statement.** Although you may not express the question in the interrogative form, you should try to embody its meaning in the introduction so that your readers have a clear idea of the purpose of the essay.

The body of the essay is the most important section. **The sole function of the body is to develop and substantiate the thesis or argument that you have stated in the introduction.** Therefore, ensure that all the ideas and examples in the body explicitly support and reinforce your thesis. The concluding paragraph sums up the major supporting points and provides a sense of closure to the essay.

There are a number of features that have to be included in your preliminary draft. These features are described in detail in other sections in the manual. Read these sections **before** commencing your draft. When writing essays on works of literature, you will frequently quote directly from the primary text. Refer to pages 87–92 for advice on using quotations. Whether your essay is based on a single primary text or on secondary sources, you need to document (or cite) any quotations or ideas borrowed from your sources. We have used parenthetical citations, a widely-used documentation style, in our sample essay on pages 17–19. Parenthetical citations are explained on pages 93–112.

Once you have completed your rough draft, you will need to revise and edit it. Allow time for revising and editing because fine-tuning the structure and polishing the style can dramatically enhance the quality of your essay. See pages 82–84 for tips on revising and editing. Converting the edited draft to the final copy is a quick and painless process. For advice on formatting the final copy, see pages 85–86. **Finally, remember to proofread your essay.**

Reflect carefully on phrasing the title of the essay and ensure that it clearly indicates to the reader the focus of your essay. Keep the title precise and concise, and use a subtitle only if it helps clarify the title. Normally the title is **not** phrased in question form.

The title page should be simple and neat. The following information is usually required on title pages for essays:

- Title
- Student name
- Course/Class
- Teacher/Instructor
- School/College/University
- Date

"Boys and Girls": A Crisis of Identity

Rick Bowness
English 4E

Mr. H. Penton
Ashbury College
December 1999

Alice Munro's "Boys and Girls" is narrated from the point of view of a woman reflecting on her years as a young girl growing up on a farm dominated by masculinity. The mother is characterized as a victim, and the father as independent and powerful. The other significant male in the story, Henry the farmhand, is brutally insensitive. Surrounded by these role models, the young girl seeks to discover her identity in a world that appears insensitive to the natural inclinations of her gender.

By portraying the mother as a tragic heroine whose integrity and spontaneity of feeling are destroyed by the traditional role she is condemned to play, Munro is commenting on the nature of the family and the damage it inflicts on the feminine spirit. The mother is forced to conform to the role of a traditional housewife, and in doing so her passion for life is undermined. Her longing, both to speak of her past and to have her daughter join her in the kitchen, underlines her isolation in a paternalistic society. It never occurred to the young girl that her mother "could be lonely or jealous" (355) because the daughter preferred what she perceived to be the "ritualistically important" outdoor work performed by her father (354). Although the mother works just as hard as the father, she receives less recognition and leads a more dependent life.

While the mother is warm and animated, the father is portrayed as cold and unfeeling — a stereotypical male. It is his duty to be tough and efficient. The young girl chooses to emulate her father rather than her mother, hoping to avoid housework so that she can work on the land as a free and independent spirit. The innocence of the young girl prevents her fully understanding the established social differences between genders, and thus she strives to fulfill the duties of manhood because they appear more adventurous. The difference between the mother and father is ruefully alluded to by the narrator as she reflects on her childhood: "My father did not talk to me unless it was about the job we were doing. In this he was quite different from my mother, who, if she were feeling cheerful, would tell me all sorts of things " (353). Munro characterizes the father as distantly silent in order to criticize the notion of the stereotypical father figure. That the young girl wishes to emulate him and not the mother emphasizes the girl's determination to avoid the traditional fate of female dependence.

The most awkward character in "Boys and Girls" is unquestionably Henry, the hired farmhand. He has "derisive eyes," spits with gusto and is able "to make his stomach growl at will" (351). The description of the scene in which he butchers a horse is as gruesomely unappealing as his personality. He is depicted as the extreme masculine stereotype, uncouth and callous, executing violent acts while remaining completely devoid of emotion. The young girl only vaguely understands his bizarre behaviour, but, as the narrator, she recalls it with disgust. While Henry's presence inhibits the emotional development of the children, he is needed to work the farm and is, therefore, considered to be more useful than the children.

In fact, the father views his own children largely in terms of their usefulness in helping to work the farm; he regards them merely as future labourers. Laird, the girl's brother, is not appreciated by his father because he lacks strength and maturity. But the mother assures the father that when "Laird gets a little bigger" the father will "have real help" (354). As the children grow older and Laird is able to help outdoors, the mother looks forward to using the daughter "more in the house" (354) — a role for the girl that her mother, having succumbed herself, clearly sees as more fitting for her daughter than working outdoors.

The young girl escapes her male-dominated world by singing and telling herself stories. "These stories were about myself" and "presented opportunities for courage, boldness and self-sacrifice" (352). These imaginative escapes give her a sense of power and freedom, but only temporarily delay that moment when she will have "to become a girl," a prospect that fills her with a feeling of "reproach and disappointment" (355). The climactic incident in the story is when she lets Flora, a horse being prepared for slaughter, escape. The narrator explains: "I did not *make any decision to do this, it was just what I did" (359). Implicit in this instinctive act is her own symbolic escape from the dependent role of a woman that she is apparently predestined to fulfill, and, at the same time, it is an affirmation of her femininity in a world dominated by silent, uncouth and seemingly heartless males.*

When, at the end, her father proclaims "with resignation, even good humour" that "she's only a girl" (360), she accepts her place in a society shaped and constrained by traditional values. But that she did not "protest" her father's declaration, "even in my heart" (360), suggests that her acceptance is not just a recognition of social reality but also a triumphant proclamation of her emerging femininity.

Work Cited

Munro, Alice. "Boys and Girls." *A 20th Century Anthology.* Eds. W.E. Messenger and W. H. New. Scarborough, ON: Prentice-Hall, 1984. 351-360.

If you are submitting an essay that is based on a single primary text, then your list of sources will consist of just that work. It is not necessary to devote a separate page to listing a single source. If you have space at the end of your essay, insert your "Work Cited" as shown above. Consult your instructor if you are in doubt.

Sketched out below are the stages that you covered in composing your essay. You will discover that, if your essay is anchored in solid preparatory work and you have followed a systematic process of outlining and drafting, the final copy not only takes less time to complete, but will be a work of superior quality.

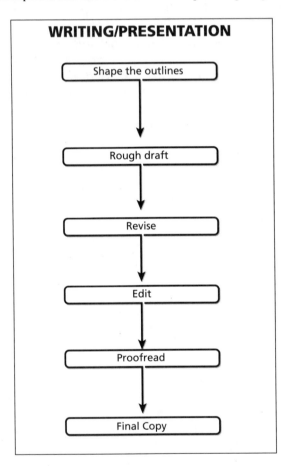

WRITING/PRESENTATION

- Shape the outlines
- Rough draft
- Revise
- Edit
- Proofread
- Final Copy

Once you have mastered the skills of writing essays focused on primary literary works — and gained self-confidence — you will find the transition to more advanced essays, such as comparisons and major research papers, far less daunting. You will also notice that the pathway you forged while writing essays on primary texts is fundamentally the same for writing comparative essays and research papers based on multiple sources.

The Comparative Essay

Introduction

A comparative assignment requires that you explain and show the significance of the similarities and/or differences present in one or more works of literature. The assignment might require you to compare two poems, or two characters from two different works, or two characters from within one work. Fundamental to the assignment will be the need to explain how a theme or themes are explored by the use of different literary techniques. Whatever the assignment might require, you must remember that it is a comparative analysis and not merely a plot summary, character description, or cataloguing of themes. **Comparisons are essays with a thesis or argument.** Traditionally, "comparing" has meant focusing just on similarities. Today, however, comparing is widely accepted as including similarities and differences. "Contrasting" means concentrating on differences only.

Let us assume that your instructor has selected two poems from the anthology you are studying and has set the following assignment for a short essay of 800–1000 words: Compare how the theme of light is represented as a regenerative force in "Composed upon Westminster Bridge" by William Wordsworth and "A Light Exists in Spring" by Emily Dickinson. Remember that "compare" allows you to focus on either similarities or differences or a combination of both. You are not required to provide citations because the assignment is based on two short poems on which the whole class is working.

Composed upon Westminster Bridge

Earth has not anything to show more fair:
Dull would he be of soul who could pass by
A sight so touching in its majesty:
This City now doth, like a garment, wear
The beauty of the morning; silent, bare,
Ships, towers, domes, theaters, and temples lie
Open unto the fields and to the sky;
All bright and glittering in the smokeless air.

Never did sun more beautifully steep
In his first splendour valley, rock, or hill;
Ne'er saw I, never felt, a calm so deep!
The river glideth at his own sweet will:
Dear God! the very houses seem asleep;
And all that mighty heart is lying still!

William Wordsworth

A Light Exists in Spring

A light exists in spring
  Not present on the year
At any other period.
  When March is scarcely here

A color stands abroad
  On solitary hills
That science cannot overtake,
  But human nature feels.

It waits upon the lawn;
  It shows the furthest tree
Upon the furthest slope we know;
  It almost speaks to me.

Then, as horizons step,
  Or noons report away,
Without the formula of sound,
  It passes, and we stay:

A quality of loss
  Affecting our content,
As trade had suddenly encroached
  Upon a sacrament.

Emily Dickinson

Preparation

Comparative assignments require that you pull together separate works or elements within a work. They may demand a little more thoughtful juggling than the single-focus essay. Therefore, some incisive preparatory reading is necessary, whether the assignment is based on two short poems or two lengthy novels. Because you have to link two elements in a comparative essay, you must have a thorough understanding of **both** works (or characters or authors) before you can start recording details.

Remember that writing essays on literary works requires that you explain how the **meaning** of a work is inextricably tied to its **form**. Begin by reading the works that you have to compare, and then list the literary devices through the prism of which you might detect the similarities and/or differences between the works. The list of devices or techniques will vary according to the literary genres that you are comparing. In our two poems, where the theme of light is similar, you might compose the following tentative list of literary devices in order to discern how the theme is explored in similar and/or different ways by the two poets.

Language	Metaphor	Symbolism	Personification
Setting	Rhythm	Point of view	Imagery
Rhyme	Mood	Irony	Tone

Using the list as a guide, you should reread the poems and isolate those devices that will be most useful in exploring how the poets develop the theme. You notice both similarities and differences in the use of language that may be helpful in explaining how each poet has dealt with the theme. You might discard rhythm and rhyme as devices for comparing the poems, and decide on tone as a more obvious method, while remaining aware that rhythm and rhyme are devices that inform the tone. After another reading of the poems, you might add mood and imagery as relevant devices for comparing the theme of light.

Once you have isolated the devices that will form the basis of your analysis, list them in your *I.Q. Journal* as shown below. Your list must represent matching categories with corresponding examples from both poems; **you cannot compare something with nothing**. This list is not necessarily final and it may change as you continue to grapple with the assignment. Such a list of similarities and differences, however, represents a tentative structure that you need **before** you start taking more comprehensive notes and structuring your outlines. You will notice from the list below that a literary device may represent both a similarity and a difference.

> ## SIMILARITIES
>
> Language   (use of literal and figurative language to describe landscapes and impressions)
>
> Mood   (a feeling of wonder in the presence of nature)
>
> Imagery   (illumination of various objects by the light)
>
> Point of view   (the first person)
>
> Tone   (use of rhythm, punctuation, diction to control tone)

> ## DIFFERENCES
>
> Language (effusive and colourful vs. stark and simple)
>
> Imagery   (highly colourful and pulsating vs. quiet and subdued)
>
> Setting   (dawn, a brief moment in time vs. the expanse of a day)
>
> Point of view (more passionately personal vs. cool and detached)
>
> Tone   (vibrant and overstated vs. restrained and understated)

Once you have a good grasp of the two poems and a tentative list of literary devices representing similarities and/or differences, you are ready to move on to the next stage. As with the primary text essay, **a system for organizing your ideas and information is crucial** for a successful comparative assignment.

Analysis is the detailed examination of your material in accordance with the question or purpose of your essay. Our analysis of the poems will, therefore, be guided by the purpose of the essay, which is to compare how the theme of light is represented as a regenerative force in "Composed on Westminster Bridge" and "A Light Exists in Spring." Not only does the purpose direct the analysis, it also shapes the list of similarities and/or differences shown on the previous page. Therefore, our tentative list of similarities and/or differences in the form of literary devices provides an analytical framework for the assignment. This structural frame allows you to classify and record relevant ideas, examples, and details from the poems, as explained on the following pages.

Using the list of literary devices on page 24 as headings, set up your notepaper pages as illustrated by the two examples below. These devices or analytical guides act as a filter to select the relevant information, ideas, and examples as you analyze your material. Simply writing down reams of notes, in the hope that some comparative links might emerge, is futile. You will notice that the note pages are arranged differently depending on whether they represent similarities or differences. There is no need to indicate after each heading whether it is a similarity or a difference because the different column arrangements make the distinction clear. CWB and LES are abbreviated versions of the titles.

Imagery

. *(The visual pictures created by the lighting up of the landscapes and the impressions they leave.)*

Language

CWB	LES
(More effusive and colourful, the words chosen to describe the city are emphatically descriptive)	*(Starker and simpler, the choice of words is not descriptively overwhelming)*

Read through the first poem, "Composed on Westminster Bridge," analyzing and dissecting as you search for examples to explain and illustrate how each device is employed to illuminate the theme. As you find details and examples representing either similarities or differences, record them under the appropriate headings, as demonstrated below. Simply use an abbreviated version of the title to indicate the source, such as CWB for "Composed on Westminster Bridge" and LES for "A Light Exists in Spring." Since you are comparing two short poems, and you are not required to provide citations, it is not necessary to indicate the line number for each note. But for longer poems and plays, you would need to provide the line number for each note, along with the source (i.e. abbreviated title), either in the margin or at the end of the note.

	Imagery
	(The visual pictures created by the lighting up of the landscapes and the impressions they leave.)
CWB	*"Earth has not anything to show more fair" (the city illuminated at dawn)*
CWB	*the illuminated city is "a sight so touching in its majesty" (suggests the impression it creates)*

	Language	
	CWB	*LES*
	(More effusive and colour-ful, the words chosen to describe the city are emphatically descriptive)	*(Starker and simpler, the choice of words is not descriptively overwhelm-ing)*
	"All bright and glittering" *"The City doth, like a gar-ment, wear/ the beauty of the morning; . . ."* *"Never did sun more beauti-fully steep . . ."*	

Then read through the other poem, probing and questioning in your search for links and connections. Record the relevant details on the appropriate note pages as explained on the previous page. You may even discover other major similarities and differences in the form of literary devices as you analyze the poems and record examples and details. Add these similarities and differences to the list in your *I.Q. Journal* and use them as a basis for unlocking more links as you read and compare the poems. Your material alone will not provide you with the similarities and/or differences — you will have to establish the connections from your own reading, questioning, and creative imagination. In this method you can write on both sides of the notepaper and you do not have to leave a line between each note.

Imagery
(The visual pictures created by the lighting up of the landscapes and the impressions they leave.)

CWB "Earth has not anything to show more fair" (the city illuminated at dawn)

CWB the illuminated city is "a sight so touching in its majesty" (suggests the impression it creates)

LES "It shows the furthest tree / Upon the furthest slope" (the distant landscape is clearly visible)

Language

CWB	LES
(More effusive and colourful, the words chosen to describe the city are emphatically descriptive)	(Starker and simpler, the choice of words is not descriptively overwhelming)
"All bright and glittering"	The light "waits upon the lawn."
"The City doth, like a garment, wear/ the beauty of the morning; . . ."	"A color stands abroad/ On solitary hills."
"Never did sun more beautifully steep . . ."	Light compared to "a sacrament"

Reread the poems slowly and then read them aloud, reflecting on how the poets depict the theme of light. Add any new ideas and information to the appropriate pages of your notes. Consider what you have done during your comparative analysis of the poems:

- You discovered examples relevant to the theme.
- You recorded these examples (with your own ideas) in note form under the appropriate headings.
- You indicated the source by using an abbreviation.

This is basically the same process for recording your notes that you followed in the primary text essay on pages 7–8. The only difference is the layout of the notepaper pages.

You will also notice in the chart below that the process for preparing a comparative essay — whether you have selected the topic and focus or whether it has been assigned by the instructor — is similar to the process followed in the single-focus primary text essay. While a comparative assignment does not require a question like the primary text essay, there are fundamental questions implied in the purpose: what are the similarities and/or differences, how are they linked, and what do they signify?

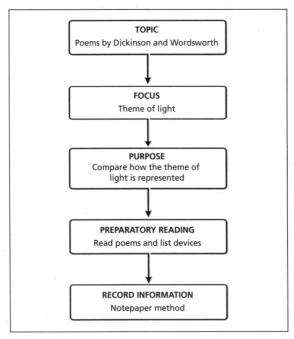

Presentation

Like the primary text essay, **a comparative essay has a thesis or point of view,** and the clarity and cogency of that thesis is shaped largely by the style of your expression and the structure of your response. Once you have completed your analysis of the poems, your notes will be grouped according to the framework of literary devices that you mapped out earlier. This list of devices affords an organizing principle that will facilitate structuring the detailed outlines.

Read through your notes carefully and decide which devices are the most significant. Do either similarities or differences dominate, or is there perhaps a balance of similarities and differences? These are important considerations because your decision will shape the thesis and the structure of the development of the thesis.

Let us assume that, in perusing our notes, we discover that the differences in how the theme of light is presented are considerably more significant than the similarities. It is logical then to focus the essay on the major differences between the two poems. In a short assignment, like this one, you may not be able to cover all the differences (or all the similarities). The next step is to select the most important differences that separate the poems to illustrate the thesis that, in their representation of light, the two poems are quite distinctive. These differences in how the poetic devices are used will form the body of the comparative essay as shown in the Basic Outline below. "(D)" indicates that the device represents a difference. Once again, **the ABC formula offers an effective structural model.**

Basic Outline

A. Introduction

B. I. Language (D)
   II. Imagery (D)
   III. Point of view (D)
   IV. Tone (D)

C. Conclusion

Once the Basic Outline is established, the next step is to structure the Skeleton Outline. Read through the notes (which will be grouped on separate pages) of each section of the Basic Outline. Then select the relevant ideas and examples needed to develop the comparison and provide supporting detail for each section. Remember that **there must be corresponding examples from both poems in order to make comparisons.** Although the structure of our example is built around differences in the depiction of light by the two poets, it may be necessary to refer briefly to minor similarities. Contrasting the paucity of similarities with the preponderance of differences emphasizes the distinctiveness of the two poems, as you will notice in the sample essay on pages 32–34.

Skeleton Outline

A. *Introduction*   *(Paragraph)*
Similar theme of regenerative effect of light
Thesis: some similar but mainly different
means of exploring it.

B. I. *Language (D)*   *(Paragraph)*
Light inspires a feeling of awe
Language to convey that feeling is different

II. *Imagery (D)*   *(Paragraph)*
Visual pictures created by the light
Sunlit picture of London at dawn
More subdued images of the light in Spring

III. *Point of view (D)*   *(Paragraph)*
Both first person personal
Wordsworth: passionate and commanding
Dickinson: quiet and tentative

IV. *Tone (D)*   *(Paragraph)*
Wordsworth: vibrant and overstated
Dickinson: restrained and understated

C. *Conclusion*   *(Paragraph)*

Once again, the outlines will provide a formula for developing the paragraphs. In a short essay, the Basic Outline establishes the paragraph structure, while the Skeleton Outline supplies the supporting details. Ensure that the **prime focus of each paragraph is on either a similarity or a difference** in the application of a specific literary device. If you wish to demonstrate that a particular literary device represents both an important similarity and a major difference, then you must create two separate paragraphs to develop each one effectively. Once you have mapped out the structure with the supporting details, it is easy to write the rough draft. Remember:

- Write clearly and correctly.
- Introduce the essay effectively.
- Organize each paragraph around a central focal point.
- Demonstrate the similarities and/or differences with corresponding examples.
- Ensure that all information and observations are relevant to your thesis.
- Sum up your conclusions in the final paragraph.
- Revise and edit the rough draft.
- Proofread the final copy.

A comparative assignment is an essay with a thesis. Therefore, you cannot just describe whatever you are comparing, such as the contents of the two poems. **You have to establish and demonstrate the links and relationships clearly** by applying the appropriate literary techniques. You cannot expect your readers to figure out the connections; that is your responsibility.

A sample comparative answer is reproduced on the following pages. You will notice that it follows closely the structure and details in the outlines. Set up your title page as shown on page 16. For example, we might title our sample essay as follows:

The Spiritual Power of Light in "Composed upon Westminster Bridge" and "A Light Exists in Spring."

The poems *"A Light Exists in Spring"* by Emily Dickinson and *"Composed upon Westminster Bridge"* by William Wordsworth both deal with the theme of how light can beautify the world. In both poems, light is represented as having a regenerative effect. While there are some similarities in language and imagery, the point of view and tone of the poems suggest, at first, a sharp difference in feeling about the power of light to renew the spirit. Not only does Wordsworth personalize his experience, but his voice is emphatic throughout, while Dickinson is more detached and apparently cool in her response to the influence of the light she sees in spring. Her subtly quiet tone, however, may well shield as intense a response to the impact of the light as Wordsworth's more effusive tone reveals.

The language of the poems, while similar in some respects, is sufficiently different to create distinctive effects. *"A color stands abroad/ On solitary hills"* evokes a feeling of awe, as does Wordsworth's *"This City now doth, like a garment, wear/ The beauty of the morning; silent, bare."* However, Wordsworth's use of a simile makes his sense of wonder more embracing and less stark than Dickinson's. Likewise, the notion that Dickinson's light in spring *"waits upon the lawn"* does not seem to carry the same weight as the morning sun rising over London *"All bright and glittering in the smokeless air."* Wordsworth imbues the sunrise over the city with the divine quality of the first light to shine on earth: *"Never did sun more beautifully steep/In his first splendour valley, rock, or hill."* Dickinson's comparison of light to a sacrament in the last stanza, while less grandiose in expression, bestows on the light a similar quality of awe and mystery.

The imagery in each poem lends to the light a similar importance but in quite different ways. Wordsworth seems to revel in the vision of the sun illuminating the great city that stretches out before him. *"Ships, towers, domes, theaters, and temples lie/ Open unto the fields and to the sky;"* — to him it is *"a sight so touching in its majesty"* that he concludes by endowing the city with *"a mighty heart."* This conclusion is not surprising since he begins his reflection on the regenerative force of light in ecstatic terms: "Earth has not anything to show more fair." These visions of a city on the brink of awakening to the vibrant pulse of life are not echoed in Dickinson's "solitary hills." In a more subdued fashion, Dickinson follows the light as it illuminates some familiar natural objects and then sinks beneath the horizon. Dickinson's spring light, however, has the same capacity to illuminate as Wordsworth's light at dawn: "It shows the furthest tree/ Upon the furthest slope." This image, unlike Wordsworth's imagery, remains discreetly uninflated.

The point of view from which the poets describe their experiences allows them to convey a sense of how they represent the theme of light. Even though Wordsworth does not use the first person until the eleventh line, he imparts the feeling that he is emotionally involved in the sight that lies before him. He almost commands the readers to share in his powerful emotions: "Dull would he be of soul who could pass by/ A sight so touching in its majesty." While Dickinson is anxious to get our attention, she does not command it. She states simply and without emotion that the quality of light in spring is quite unusual. When she herself enters the poem it is tentatively: "It [the light] almost speaks to me." At the end she merges into the crowd by explaining how the "loss" of the light affects "our content," not just hers, thereby inviting us to share her feelings without imposing them on us. Wordsworth's response, on the other hand, is deeply personal: "Ne'er saw I, never felt, a calm so deep!" Just as we are commanded to share in his sense of wonder at what the sun illuminates, so are we passionately encouraged to experience with him his intense feeling of serenity inspired by the vision.

The contrasting points of view that the poets adopt towards their descriptions of the effect of the light are reflected in the tones of voice that they assume. Wordsworth's intensely personal response is made evident through his use of overstatement, whereas Dickinson's more detached, less effusive response employs understatement. The last four lines of "Composed upon Westminster Bridge" contain three exclamation marks; none can be found in "A Light Exists in Spring." Dickinson's seemingly quiet voice, however, may cover up an equally intense response. While she never exclaims "Dear God!" as Wordsworth does, she is nonetheless awestruck by the supernatural power of the light "That science cannot overtake,/ But human nature feels." The strength of her feelings, communicated in a reserved tone of voice, is not as readily apparent as that of Wordsworth's. He punctuates his feelings in a voice that seems to vibrate.

The two poems describe how the power of light can be a regenerative force. Wordsworth's more vivid use of language, his more glaringly revealed images, and more emphatic voice make his feelings about the force of the sun illuminating London at dawn much more immediate. He leaves no doubt that his spirits have been revived. "A Light Exists in Spring" does not set out to enthral us in the same way but, with a style that is soft and gentle, impresses on us the power that light has to touch us deeply.

Once again, the process of structuring and composing your comparative essay is no different from the stages you covered in composing the single-focus primary text essay.

Shape the outlines → Rough draft → Revise → Edit → Proofread → Final copy

Comparative assignments in literature tend to focus on primary text analysis. Major comparative research papers involving the use of secondary critical sources are usually only required in advanced university courses. Whether you are assigned a short comparative essay on two characters in a single primary text, or whether you are required to undertake a major comparative research paper based on supplementary secondary sources, the process and the organization are similar. **The advantage of a well-defined pathway is that it can be easily modified for use in a variety of assignments.**

The Research Paper

Introduction

The research paper takes you into another realm of writing about literature. While it still requires that you focus on primary texts, the argument, thesis, or point of view that you present will have to be substantiated through the use of supplementary primary sources and secondary critical sources, as well as your own thoughtful and imaginative insights.

Your research may take you in many interesting directions. For example, you may be able to place a work of literature in its historical context and examine the impact that it had on its time. You may discover in secondary sources various interpretations of a single work of literature that you can attempt to resolve. On the other hand, you may wish to proceed in a more theoretical direction and subject a work to a specific critical approach, such as psychological or archetypal. You will discover in your studies that the opportunities for exploring and writing about literature are almost limitless.

Research is not simply digging for information. **Research includes both creative and critical thinking in a process of systematic investigation.** Developing new ideas and insights is as important as finding new information and data. And, as important as the research process is, the ability to convey your responses and interpretations to the reader in a clear and logical manner is equally important.

Finally, remember that a research paper is an essay, and like the primary text essay, it has your response imprinted on it in the form of a thesis, argument, or point of view.

Preparing the Paper

SELECTING THE TOPIC

Frequently, instructors will ask you to select your own topic. Being involved in the project from the outset confers a sense of ownership and invariably creates a heightened degree of engagement, commitment, and interest. Let us assume that you are studying selected works of Russian literature in translation and your instructor has asked you to choose the topic for your term paper. After reflecting on the course outline and the reading list and carefully considering your own literary interests, you select the plays of Anton Chekhov as the broad topic you wish to explore.

Discuss your choice of topic with the instructor and clarify items such as the following:

- The number of sources to be used.

- Whether the sources should include both primary and secondary sources.

- Whether a specific critical approach is required.

- The citation or documentation procedures required.

- The length of the completed paper.

- The due date and whether there is a penalty for late submission.

- The overall structure, such as the nature of the introduction and the conclusion.

- Matters of style, such as the use of the first person.

- Format and layout for the final copy.

- The criteria for assessment and whether a sample evaluation form is available.

As soon as the due date is established, **start planning a schedule for the completion of the various stages of the paper.** Planning requires a practical process or pathway with clearly defined stages of development, such as those outlined opposite, coupled with a careful allotment of time.

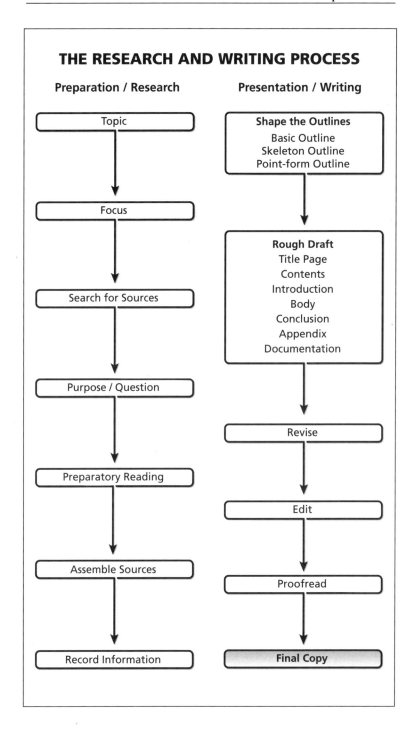

THE RESEARCH AND WRITING PROCESS

Preparation / Research **Presentation / Writing**

Topic	Shape the Outlines
Focus	Rough Draft
Search for Sources	Revise
Purpose / Question	Edit
Preparatory Reading	Proofread
Assemble Sources	Final Copy
Record Information	

Topic → Focus → Search for Sources → Purpose / Question → Preparatory Reading → Assemble Sources → Record Information

Shape the Outlines
Basic Outline
Skeleton Outline
Point-form Outline

Rough Draft
Title Page
Contents
Introduction
Body
Conclusion
Appendix
Documentation

Revise

Edit

Proofread

Final Copy

NARROWING THE FOCUS

Narrowing the topic to a specific focus is as important in a major research paper as it is in a shorter essay on a primary text. However, a research paper, unlike a shorter essay based solely on a primary text, will require exploratory reading that may take you into sources such as surveys of literature, encyclopedias and biographical dictionaries. The library catalogue and indexes at the back of books and encyclopedias may provide interesting leads. In addition, you might consult the *Library of Congress Subject Headings* and periodical and newspaper indexes, which are explained in the Appendix. A preliminary search of the Internet will likely turn up stimulating ideas. For example, "The Anton Chekhov Page" lists dozens of interesting possibilities. Viewing films and television documentaries on your topic could also suggest new ideas. Once again, you will be looking for the major features, issues, and aspects that could serve as an interesting and challenging focus for exploration. As with the earlier essays, use your *I.Q. Journal* to list your ideas, questions, and comments.

Narrowing the topic is a crucial stage in the research process because the issue, aspect or feature that you select will provide the focus for your investigation. It is important to devote your attention to an issue that is not too broad and not too narrow. You should also avoid issues that lend themselves to a largely narrative, descriptive or biographical approach. Remember that the purpose of an academic essay is not to retell a story or rephrase a text. Controversial issues and contentious interpretations can work well because they are usually widely written about and vigorously debated. They provide an opportunity to test conflicting perspectives and values, and enable you to leave **your personal imprint** on the completed essay.

Frequently, this narrowing or focusing process will involve more than one stage. If you had chosen the plays of Anton Chekhov as your topic, you might decide to focus on the role of the female characters in his plays. You might then discover that this emphasis is still too broad unless you focus on the female characters in a specific play such as *Uncle Vanya*.

SEARCHING FOR SOURCES

Once you have decided on a specific focus for your essay, the next step is to compile a list of potential sources of information.* It is important to **determine as soon as possible whether there are sufficient sources available** on the issue that you intend to investigate. If not, you will have to substitute your second choice.

Libraries can appear overwhelming, but there is no need to panic. If introductory tours are available, start by signing up for a tour of your library and later wander around on your own, familiarizing yourself with the layout. Many libraries provide handouts on everything from regulations to lists of reference materials. Develop a collection of these information sheets and read them carefully. Approach the library staff if you have difficulties. They are the specialists with the expertise to answer your questions. Their advice and suggestions will save hours of your time.

A great variety of source material is available and most libraries have a wide array of searching techniques to trace this material. To avoid diverting you from the research process by describing these techniques in detail here, they have been placed in the Appendix. Read pages 121–126 carefully once you are familiar with the research process. Do not be intimidated by the range of research resources. You are likely to use only a few of these resources initially. As you undertake research assignments during your high school and university years, try to familiarize yourself with as many of these resources as possible. Test them out in your library: hands-on, practical experience is a far better teacher than a manual. Knowing which resources exist in your research field will not only save time but will allow you to build a wide-ranging list of sources. And, of course, a knowledge of the various research aids will make it easier for you to prepare subsequent assignments in many different subjects.

---

* You may wish to define the precise purpose of your essay before searching for sources. If so, merely reverse the next two stages, "Searching for Sources" and "Defining the Purpose" (pages 45–46).

As you work through the research aids, you will be searching for sources relevant to your issue — the focus of your research. This preliminary list of sources is known as your **Working Bibliography**. As you find relevant references, simply list the authors, titles, and publication details of the sources, as shown on the next page. There is no need to locate and assemble the material at this stage because you are primarily determining the availability of potential material, and you may not even have decided on the precise purpose of the essay yet. It is unlikely that someone will clean out the library holdings on your topic because many sources are now in electronic form, and others, such as reference works and periodicals, may not leave the library. Furthermore, searching techniques have made a greater volume of source material available, so there is usually less pressure on limited library resources today.

Enter all the publication details for each source accurately because these details will be required for the final list of sources (Works Cited or Bibliography). If you do this conscientiously, there will be no need to check the source details later, wasting valuable time. Neither is there any need to write up these details in final format at this stage. However, if you wish to enter the details in a specific documentary style in your Working Bibliography, consult your instructor to determine the required style for the essay. You will notice in our examples on the following pages that we have used two styles, with only minor differences, to illustrate how to set up a Working Bibliography. These styles — Modern Language Association and Chicago/Turabian — are discussed on pages 93–95.

Although the entries in the final Bibliography or Works Cited are listed alphabetically, do not attempt at this stage to place your preliminary sources in alphabetical order. Concentrate on building a diversified range of sources and list the relevant publication details accurately.

There are three recommended methods for building the Working Bibliography: you can use standard notepaper, index cards or a computer. The bibliographic information can be listed in exactly the same way in all three methods, as demonstrated on the next three pages. Choose the method that best suits your needs.

Notepaper Method

As you discover potential sources of information, list them on standard notepaper and fill in all the essential bibliographic details as follows:

Working Bibliography

FP — Chekhov, Anton. *Five Plays.* Trans. Ronald Hingley. New York: Oxford UP, 1977.

CP — Gilman, Richard. *Chekhov's Plays: An Opening into Eternity.* New Haven, CT: Yale UP, 1995. (University library, PG3458.28G5)

CA — "Chekhov, Anton." *Britannica.com.* 1999. By Ronald Hingley. *Encyclopaedia Britannica.* 15 Nov. 1999 http://www.britannica.com/bcom/eb/article/0/0,5716,23120 3,00.html .

- Continue listing all your sources in this manner.

- The codes (e.g. FP and CP) represent abbreviated forms of the titles. Codes are used to identify sources during the research.

- Enter the library location and call number once you know where the source is held.

Index Card Method

As you discover potential sources of information, list them on separate index cards and fill in all the essential bibliographic details as follows:

FP

Chekhov, Anton. Five Plays. Translated by Ronald Hingley.
New York: Oxford University Press, 1977.

CP

Gilman, Richard. Chekhov's Plays: An Opening into Eternity.
New Haven, CT: Yale University Press, 1995.
(University library, PG3458.28G5)

- Continue listing all your sources in this manner.

- The codes (e.g. FP and CP) represent abbreviated forms of the titles. Codes are used to identify sources during the research.

- Enter the library location and call number once you know where the source is held.

Computer Method

Computer technology is transforming researching techniques. You can use computers to search for sources, compile the Working Bibliography, and store the researched information. Using a computer and a modem, you can search library holdings and databases throughout the world. Electronic searching is explained on pages 121–122 in the Research Aids section of the Appendix. You can copy the sources manually from the screen onto index cards or notepaper, as illustrated on the previous two pages; alternatively, you can have the computer transfer the information to a Working Bibliography file and print it later.

You can also search manually for your sources in the various research aids in the library and then, using a portable computer and a word processing program, you can set up a Working Bibliography file and enter the publication details as shown on page 41. Software programs allow you to create your own electronic index cards, if you prefer cards to notepaper for your Working Bibliography.

The range and calibre of your sources can dramatically enhance the quality of your essays. When designing a search strategy for developing your Working Bibliography, try to balance books and articles, electronic and audio-visual information, old and new material, conservative and radical interpretations and primary and secondary sources. To expand the diversity of your sources you can classify them in groups such as Books, Articles, Audio-Visual, Electronic and Primary. You can then use different coloured index cards, such as blue for books and yellow for articles, to identify the different categories of sources. Enter the details as shown on page 42. If you are using notepaper for your Working Bibliography, you can classify your sources in a similar way by devoting a separate page to each category. For example, head a page "Books," and then write in the details for each book as shown on page 41.

If you are searching electronically, you can print your sources and cut and paste them onto coloured cards or pages of notepaper. Alternatively, you can copy the sources to disk instead of printing them. Then you can create separate files for the different categories, such as Books and Articles, and transfer the sources to the appropriate files. You can print them later if necessary. Whichever computer method you are using to search and list your sources, make sure to record exact addresses or use bookmarks so that you can locate the sources again.

You may wish to devise your own set of classified headings to extend the range of your sources. There is a rich vein of material available today and a variety of techniques to trace it. Combine tradition and technology with tenacity in combing the many resources. Careful use of these resources and frequent practice will save you hours of frustrated searching, and you will be surprised at the quantity of information you can assemble on almost any topic. You will undoubtedly experience obstacles in digging for material, but do not give up: the persistent researcher is invariably rewarded.

Once you have assured yourself that there are adequate sources available to develop your essay, move on to the next stage. The length of your Working Bibliography will be determined either by the nature of the assignment or by the instructor. For most high school and university papers, a preliminary list of eight to fifteen sources should be adequate. If, despite intensive searching, you find an insufficient number of sources, you will have to select another issue from the backup list in your *I.Q. Journal*. **Make the change at this early stage**. It is frustrating to discover as the deadline approaches that there are insufficient sources to build a paper. By determining the extent of potential sources at this early stage of the process, you will avoid the agony of having to find another issue and start anew with the deadline looming.

Another advantage of developing the Working Bibliography in the early stages of the project is that interesting possibilities might emerge that may serve as the purpose of the essay. Abstracts, titles and subtitles of sources often suggest challenging research questions. Jot any interesting ideas down in your *I.Q. Journal*.

DEFINING THE PURPOSE

Once you have narrowed your topic to an important issue or aspect and established that there are sufficient sources of information, the next step is to define more precisely the direction of your research. You can give a clear sense of direction to your essay — whether it is based on a single primary text or on multiple sources — by launching it with an incisive and challenging question. This is a crucial stage because the question spells out your purpose: your quest is in the question.

The research question also refines the focus and defines the scope of the essay. If you are expected to produce a short paper, do not get carried away and pose a question that would produce a book. If the question is clear and precise, it will give direction and purpose to the assignment. Your sole task is to answer the question. **The answer will form your thesis, argument, or point of view**.

Since your goal is to develop a thesis or argument, you should avoid questions that lead to biographical, narrative or descriptive answers, such as "Who was Flannery O'Connor?" or "How does romantic poetry differ from epic poetry?" Also, do not pose speculative or hypothetical questions such as "Would Alice Munro's stories be different if she had grown up in the American South?" There can be no conclusive answers to such conjectures.

Always try to formulate a **single,** challenging question that demands analysis and argument — a question that can be stated precisely and succinctly in just one sentence. Avoid compound or multiple questions, such as "How do dialogue, the description of settings, and the employment of interior monologue underpin the thematic development and mood of Virginia Woolf's *To the Lighthouse?*" because they invariably create confusion. "Why" questions, such as "Why is sensual imagery in Keats' poetry essential to its effectiveness?" work well because they lend themselves to clear, structured answers, and they usually avoid the biographical, narrative or descriptive trap. In addition, they also give a well-defined focus and direction to your research.

Frequently, you will have discovered interesting ideas, perspectives and questions while building your Working Bibliography. Further brainstorming sessions with fellow students can help expand your range of interesting and innovative options. If you still have difficulty in designing a good question, it may be necessary to do additional reading on the focus of your research. Gather as many potential questions as possible and list them in your *I.Q. Journal.* Think carefully before making your final decision and then check with the instructor to ensure that your research question is acceptable and appropriately phrased.

Let us return to our example of the female characters in *Uncle Vanya.* If our interest is in their roles in the play, we might formulate the question as follows: Why are the female characters important in *Uncle Vanya?* The direction of the essay is clearly set. **Your task is to answer the question — that is the sole purpose of the assignment.**

There is an alternative method for launching your research. Some manuals suggest initiating the process of preparing an essay by proposing a thesis or tentative theory. But jumping from the broad topic to a statement of thesis or argument is a quantum leap that can be confusing and intimidating for many students. Another difficulty with this approach is that you must have the background knowledge to suggest a sound thesis or hypothesis as a starting point. Furthermore, there is the temptation to select material to support your position, while rejecting material that runs counter to it.* Launching your essay with a precise, open-ended question, such as "Why are Alice Munro's short stories about rural Ontario of interest to an international readership?" opens up a wider range of possibilities than starting from a fixed position, such as "Alice Munro's fictional technique is responsible for her broad readership." It might be useful to remember Sherlock Holmes' advice: never theorize in advance of the facts.

---

*Certain types of assignments, usually in the social sciences, do lend themselves to launching the research process with a hypothesis or proposition. However, avoid starting your research with an "educated guess" and then selecting information "to prove the thesis." It is intellectual dishonesty to consciously select material to support a predetermined position, while ignoring information that contradicts it.

PREPARATORY READING

Once you have defined the purpose of your essay, you need to develop a better understanding of the focus of your investigation before you start the detailed research. **The emphasis of an academic paper written on a literary topic must be on the primary text.** Acquaint yourself thoroughly with the literary text that is the subject of your analysis — if you have not already done so — before starting to read widely in secondary sources.

It is likely that you have already read the primary text as part of the earlier exploratory reading. Rereading the primary text is time well spent because each reading will unlock additional ideas, insights and responses. You will not have the time to reread lengthy works such as *War and Peace,* so it is advisable to choose works of moderate length on which to base your essays initially.

While you are engaged in the preparatory reading, keep the question or purpose of the essay uppermost in your mind. Be guided by your purpose as you jot down your reactions and responses. Elements of an argument or thesis may start to emerge. Likewise, a tentative structure might start to appear. Note these responses and ideas in your *I.Q. Journal.*

You are not doing formal research at this stage; you are undertaking the preparatory reading to acquaint yourself with the text and the author, and to reflect on the focus and the question. Guided by the question, you are gauging your emotional and intellectual responses to the text. All readers bring their own emotional and intellectual backgrounds to their encounters with a text, and there is no telling in advance what sparks — if any — will fly as a result of these encounters. A careful reading can trigger genuinely fresh insights and responses, especially in the light of a thoughtful question.

The preparatory reading is more focused and directed than the earlier exploratory and preliminary reading. In addition to the primary text, your preparatory reading could also include some of the reference works, such as encyclopedias, biographical dictionaries, and general surveys of literature that you may have used for the exploratory and preliminary reading. You might even locate a few of the shorter sources from your Working Bibliography and read them quickly. Pre-reading some of your sources will provide you with an overview of the content before you start recording the details, and will also enable you to determine whether a particular source has any merit. **Remember, however, that the primary text is of paramount importance in the preparatory reading.**

Investing your time in the preparatory reading is well worth it because you are "preparing" yourself for an important stage of the research: analyzing your material and recording the relevant information, insights, and ideas needed to develop your argument or thesis. The preparatory reading will provide you with the background knowledge needed to develop perceptive questions, and will help you judge what is relevant, reliable and important in the answers. Much of your reading and brainstorming — and even some of your research notes — never appear in the final copy. But like the nine tenths of an iceberg that is below the surface of the water, they form the invisible foundations that keep the essay afloat. Set aside time for the preparatory work in your scheduling — **the more time and effort expended initially in preparing the essay, the less is needed later in writing the essay**.

During the preparatory reading, you might discover another aspect of your topic that is more interesting and challenging than your original choice. If the alternative issue is more compelling than the original, do not hesitate to change direction by shifting the focus and formulating another question. The change may be as minor as modifying the research question. For example, after reading *Uncle Vanya*, you might rephrase the question as follows: How do the female characters shape the mood in *Uncle Vanya*?

The research pathway is flexible and adaptable, so do not hesitate to change direction and alter the focus or fine-tune the question. Ensure, however, that the sources in your Working Bibliography remain relevant to any changes in the focus or the question. You cannot afford the time to revise your Working Bibliography at this stage of the project. It is also advisable to consult your instructor about any proposed changes.

RECORDING INFORMATION AND IDEAS

Armed with a thorough understanding of your subject from your preparatory reading, a substantial list of sources, and an incisive question, you are now ready to start analyzing your material and recording the relevant information and ideas. **The preliminary work is essential: there are no shortcuts to success.**

First, you have to locate and assemble your sources. Do not panic if you cannot find all the sources listed in your Working Bibliography, as it is unlikely that they will all be available in your community libraries. That is why you originally listed more sources than you really needed. The number of sources that you actually use may be determined by the instructor, by the scope of the essay, or by the length of the sources themselves. You should be able to complete a high school or university research paper with between five and ten sources. As you track down a source, note the library location and catalogue number (if you have not done so already) in your Working Bibliography so that you can find it again easily if necessary.

Using a variety of source material will improve your essay. A source may be biased, unbalanced, or even erroneous. By consulting a number of sources, you gain access to a wider range of interpretations and information. Frequently, you will encounter conflicting information, and a wider range of sources will often enable you to confirm (or reject) controversial information. To avoid diverting you from the explanation of the research process in this section, the nature, use and evaluation of sources have been placed in the Appendix. Read pages 127–131 once you are comfortable with the research process.

Remember that your task is to develop a thoughtful and convincing answer to your research question. Whether you are writing an essay based on a single primary text or on multiple sources, a systematic method for recording your information and ideas is essential. It is worth remembering the Chinese proverb that the palest ink is better than the most retentive memory.

Research involves analyzing, selecting, and recording information and ideas. Analysis means breaking something down into its smaller elements. Analysis involves a careful examination and dissection of your material and the identification and isolation of details and ideas in accordance with the purpose of your assignment. As you read through your sources, examine the material carefully and extract the important information and ideas (the "smaller elements") that are relevant to your research question. Once you have selected the relevant details and ideas, record them in your research notes. **The research question guides your research.** The question directs the analysis, the selection and the recording of the evidence.

Research in the humanities is not a mechanical gathering of "facts." It is a complex process requiring both creative imagination and critical thought. You have to dissect your material and evaluate interpretations and judgments as you systematically search for an answer to your research question. Read critically: do not accept ideas and interpretations blindly. Be skeptical: read between the lines and beyond the print. Question continuously as you read and examine carefully the arguments and opinions of the authors. **Raise your own stimulating and challenging questions; they can yield surprising new insights**.

Take special care in the way you select information and ideas to record in your notes — to look for information just to "prove" a preconceived position or thesis is biased research. Biased research is both suspect and unethical. You should consider all perspectives and approaches to your question and record all relevant information and interpretations, whether they support or contradict your personal position on the issue that you are investigating.

There are four main types of notes:

- Direct quotations.
- Personal insights, responses, questions, and comments.
- Paraphrasing information and ideas.
- Summarizing information and ideas.

Reading, analyzing, selecting, and recording the evidence that you will need to develop your point of view or thesis is a major part of preparing research papers. Allow at least one third of the overall time that you have set aside to produce your paper for this important stage.

Itemized below are some suggestions to assist you in compiling your notes:

- Try to pre-read your sources and then reread them and record your notes.

- Be concise, clear and accurate.

- Use the table of contents and index in each book so that you can save time by focusing on the relevant pages only.

- Add your own ideas, comments, and questions; do not just quote, summarize or paraphrase.

- If you develop your own shorthand system for recording notes, ensure that your abbreviations and symbols will make sense to you later.

- Use your own words where possible.

- Transcribe direct quotations accurately, enclosing them in quotation marks.

- Use quotations mainly from the primary text, rather than from secondary sources.

- Record all the essential information so that you do not have to consult your sources again when composing the essay.

- Indicate whether a piece of evidence is established fact or subjective opinion.

- Material may be interesting and it may true, but ask yourself if it is relevant to your question or purpose.

- Plagiarism is the unacknowledged use of someone else's ideas. Identifying the sources of all your notes can help you avoid charges of plagiarism.

- If you find new sources, add them to your Working Bibliography.

You can use notepaper, index cards, or a computer to record information and ideas. In the primary text and the comparative essays we used the notepaper method to illustrate the recording process. This time we will use index cards to demonstrate the process. The smallest size of index card is recommended for your notes.

Index Card Method

The detailed analysis must start with the primary text. *Uncle Vanya* was subjected to an initial reading, and perhaps even a second reading, during the preliminary research or pre-writing process. Now it must be carefully perused and analyzed to isolate the ideas, examples, and information that will enable you to develop an answer to the research question.

As you read through *Uncle Vanya* in the anthology *Five Plays,* you notice a reference in the play to the role of the female characters. Since this point is relevant to the research question, you record it on an index card as shown on the next page. Before recording the point you must decide what type of note to use. Most of your quoted notes (notes containing direct quotations) will be from the primary text because you will need verbatim excerpts to support your interpretations and insights. Each quoted note should be accompanied by a bracketed comment or observation, as shown on the sample card opposite.

You must identify the source of the note or quotation in case you need to refer to it for further details or you need to acknowledge the source in a citation. It is unnecessary to record all the publication details, such as author, title, and publisher on each note card. Simply use the code that stands for an abbreviated form of the title, as explained on pages 41–42. For example, "FP" stands for *Five Plays* by Chekhov. In addition to the source, you must also indicate the page reference for the information. Therefore, "FP 142" indicates that the quotation is from page 142 of *Five Plays* as shown on the sample card on the next page. In similar fashion to the recording process for the primary text essay on pages 7–8, you have:

- Discovered relevant information pertaining to the research question.
- Recorded it in a quoted note.
- Indicated the source and page number.

There is one minor difference between the single text essay and the multiple source research essay: you have added the code to identify the specific source.

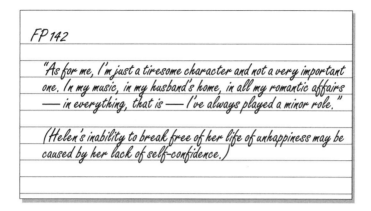

Continue reading through the primary text, looking for ideas and information relevant to the research question. If a development in the play triggers an observation and a specific quotation is not necessary to accompany it, just summarize the point as shown below, indicating the code and page reference.

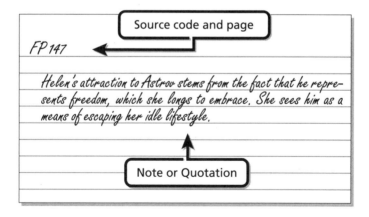

Work through the primary text questioning, analyzing, selecting, and recording the relevant information. **A close and engaged interaction with the text should ensure a continuous flow of ideas and insights.** Once you have completed a thorough reading of the primary text, and you have recorded detailed notes on your cards, check it off in your Working Bibliography, and move on to the next source.

Take your next source, Richard Gilman's book *Chekhov's Plays: An Opening into Eternity,* which you have coded "CP." Read through source CP, looking specifically for information pertaining to the question. Record the details on separate cards as previously explained, either as a quotation, a summary or a paraphrase, adding your own comments, responses, and questions, as shown below.

CP 111

The power of Uncle Vanya comes from the fact that these characters seem real; they are not symbols which we must decipher, but rather we see these characters and we see our own experiences.

CP119

" . . . to say that one is bored more often than not masks another condition, one more painful or dangerous to announce: distress, embarrassment, anger, grief, or fear."

(Helen's idleness is actually repressed misery. Her constant complaints of boredom are her way of avoiding her real feelings, such as her affection for Astrov.)

And so you continue consulting all your available sources — whether they are primary or secondary, oral or online — searching for ideas and information relevant to your purpose or question, and then systematically record the details and identify the sources on separate index cards.

Bear these points in mind when you are using index cards:

- Do not confuse bibliographic cards, that list sources, with note cards, that contain ideas and information.

- Each note card should contain two items:

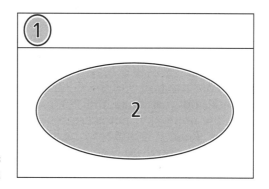

  1. Source code and page.
  2. Note.

- Write just one note on each card.

- Use the smallest index cards. It is easier to shape your outlines with small cards, each containing just one major point.

- Your research cards have no special order and, as they are all independent, there is no need to number them.

- Finish writing a long note on the reverse side of the card rather than continuing on another card.

- Use cards for diagrams, such as a genealogical chart for understanding family relationships in a novel.

- Use your initials as the source code when recording personal insights and comments.

- You may also use coloured cards to distinguish different types of cards. For example, you might use white cards for research notes and blue cards for bibliographic details. (If you colour-coded your Working Bibliography as explained on page 43, then do not use coloured cards as suggested here.)

- Once you have completed using a source, write critical comments on the reverse side of the bibliographic card. These comments can be used to compile an annotated bibliography for your essay.

- Use a file box or two-ring card folder to hold your cards.

Notepaper Method

Instead of using index cards, you can use notepaper to record your ideas, examples, and information in the same manner, as explained on pages 7–9 for the primary text essay. The only difference is that here you have to add a code to the page reference to identify the specific source because you are using multiple sources for your research paper. There are also only minor differences between the index card method and the notepaper method. The notepaper method just links the "index cards" together. Later, when the notepaper notes are separated, the difference disappears. Read pages 52–54 because they contain relevant information about notemaking techniques.

Set up your notepaper recording system as described on page 7 and record your information in a similar manner, identifying each note with a source code and page reference. Remember to leave a blank line between each note and write on one side of the page only. This method uses a different page layout than the recording system for the comparative essay where each notepage had a literary device as a heading; otherwise, the process is similar.

FP 142	"As for me, I'm just a tiresome character and not a very important one. In my music, in my husband's home, in all my romantic affairs — in everything, that is — I've always played a minor role." (Helen's inability to break free of her life of unhappiness may be caused by her lack of self-confidence.)
FP 147	Helen's attraction to Astrov stems from the fact that he represents freedom, which she longs to embrace. She sees him as a means of escaping her idle lifestyle.
FP 150	Helen, at the moment of decision, succumbs to her inertia and rejects Astrov, although not without some hesitation.

Computer Method

Recording your information and ideas with a computer is also an option. If you prefer using a computer, you should still read pages 52–56 because the notemaking techniques for index cards and notepaper also apply to computer usage. If you prefer the notepaper method, you can set up a word processor file for your notes. If you prefer index cards, there are software packages that will allow you to write, edit, retrieve, and sort "cards" on the screen. Record the details, identify the sources, and follow the procedures described earlier.

Modems and networks are providing quick and easy access to library holdings and other databases. The information in these databases is often in a variety of formats, such as text, video, sound, graphics, and photographs. You can browse and "import" information in text or graphic form directly to your note file, but **remember the warning about plagiarism** when downloading from electronic sources.

Whatever research method you use, remember to keep these points in mind:

- Allow enough time in your schedule for preparing your essay. You need adequate time to read, research, respond, reflect, and record.

- The research question directs the analysis, the selection, and the recording process.

- A comprehensive and organized system of notes is essential. It is exceedingly difficult to write an intelligent essay without good notes.

- The process described is not a rigid straightjacket; it is flexible. Modify it and shape a research pathway to suit your needs.

- Think and question continuously as you read, and list your responses and insights in your *I.Q. Journal* or in your notes. Your questions may be more important than the answers.

Writing the Paper

INTRODUCTION

Now that the analysis and the recording have been completed, you can start shaping and composing your answer to the research question. The analysis is one side of the process, the synthesis is the other side. As with the primary text essay, your answer or response represents **your argument, point of view, or thesis** — it is the glue that holds the essay together. Once again, the clarity of your answer is your prime objective, and that clarity is largely a function of the structure of your argument and the style of your expression.

In addition to practical matters of structure and style, there are philosophical issues, such as interpretation, selection, subjectivity, and bias, that have to be addressed. In writing about works of literature, our responses are governed by our intellects and emotions, by our heads and hearts. Unlike the social sciences, with their emphasis on empirical data, our perceptions and responses to literature are conditioned primarily by our emotions, our backgrounds, and by the knowledge we derive from our own experiences. Reading literary works through the prism of our own identity necessarily tints the spectacles with which we interpret those works. Consider how differently a student from an urban ghetto and another from an affluent suburb would interpret a novel about social class.

The selection process, an inescapable aspect of preparing an essay, is also affected by our subjective perspective. In selecting and narrowing the topic, and developing a Working Bibliography, you had to make choices. You selected certain sources from your Working Bibliography, and then from your reading and analysis of these sources you selected your notes. You will be making further selections from your notes to create your outlines. Subjective identity influences every stage of the selection process — a process that is crucial in preparing your essay, because you are presenting a personal point of view or argument that is shaped and supported by selected evidence.

While it is difficult to escape subjectivity, we must be meticulous in the way we evaluate our sources and critical about how we select our supporting evidence. It may be difficult to remain impartial on some emotionally charged issues, but we must strive at all times to be fair and honest researchers and writers. That means we must avoid bias. Bias is a consciously partisan selection of information to promote a preconceived point of view.[4] Bias is prejudging an issue, and that is prejudice. **Bias is unethical and unacceptable. Subjectivity is innate and unavoidable.**

Since subjectivity pervades all aspects of writing about literature, unanimity of interpretation is rare. You will encounter a range of equally valid opinions and theories amongst authorities and even amongst your peers. There is no final proof and no ultimate truth in literary studies.

SHAPING THE OUTLINES

Discipline and structure are necessary for successful expression, and form and order are essential elements in achieving clarity of expression. As was explained for the primary text essay, the ABC formula provides a simple and effective structural model for promoting clear communication.

Once you have completed your reading and recording, your notes will be organized on index cards, notepaper or computer. It is impossible to write a final copy straight from these notes. A number of intermediate stages are necessary to ensure quality. Shaping the structure of the essay is your next task. The following section on outlining demonstrates the importance of organization in developing clarity of argument **before** you start to draft your essay.

Before creating your detailed outlines, you should read ahead about the roles of the introduction, body and conclusion on pages 69–78. Since you may have to counter alternative interpretations, you should read about opposing viewpoints on pages 67 and 73. You should also reread the section on the use of quotations on pages 87–92. All these features and details will have to be included in your outlines.

Basic Outline

Allow yourself **time** to reread your notes and to reflect on the ideas in your *I.Q. Journal* while keeping the research question uppermost in your mind. Try to isolate the main factors around which you can structure an answer in the body of the essay. You may even have a tentative list of possible factors that you jotted down in your *I.Q. Journal* during the course of the preparatory reading and the research. We have isolated four main factors around which to develop our answer to the question, "How do the female characters shape the mood in *Uncle Vanya?*" This list of main factors is called the Basic Outline.

Basic Outline

A. Introduction

B. I. Relationships with male characters
   II. Relationships with female characters
   III. Reaction to the surroundings
   IV. The future

C. Conclusion

Once you have created your Basic Outline, read through your note cards again and arrange them in groups corresponding to the outline. The next step is to number the cards according to the sections of the Basic Outline into which they fall. For instance, all notes dealing with relationships with the male characters are labeled "I" because "Relationships with male characters" is section I of the body of the Basic Outline above. Use the upper right-hand corner of each index card for the section number, as shown in the example at the top of the next page. Once you have finished assigning numbers to your cards, arrange them in their groups in a file box, a two-ring card folder, or use rubber bands to group them.

> *FP 147*   */*
>
> *Helen's attraction to Astrov stems from the fact that he rep-*
> *resents freedom, which she longs to embrace. She sees him as*
> *a means of escaping her idle lifestyle.*

If you used notepaper, separate the individual notes with scissors as explained on page 12 and demonstrated below. In effect, you have created separate "cards" out of your pages of notes.

> *FP*   *Helen's attraction to Astrov stems from the fact*   */*
> *147* *that he represents freedom, which she longs to*
>   *embrace. She sees him as a means of escaping her*
>   *idle lifestyle.*

If you used a computer to record your material, you might find it easier at this stage to print copies of your notes and organize them manually, as described above. If you used "electronic notepaper," you can create separate files for each section of the Basic Outline, and then transfer the individual notes to the appropriate files. If you used index card software, sort and group your "cards" electronically, as explained on the bottom of the previous page.

Remember to ensure that all sections of the Basic Outline address the question and to reject any irrelevant notes as explained on page 12 in the section dealing with the primary text essay.

Skeleton Outline

The Basic Outline provides the overall structure of your essay. To move from the Basic Outline to the more detailed Skeleton Outline, read carefully through the notes of each section of the Basic Outline, identifying the important subsections. The advantage of index cards or notepaper strips is that you can take a section at a time and spread the strips or cards on a table, move them around and then map out the substructure for each section. This stage, containing the main sections with their subsections, is the Skeleton Outline.

Skeleton Outline

A. Introduction
    Background
    Focus
    Purpose
    Thesis

B. I. Relationships with male characters
        1. tension increased by Helen's presence
        2. Sonya offers comfort

    II. Relationships with female characters
        1. Helen and Sonya make peace
        2. Helen tries to help Sonya

    III. Reaction to surroundings
        1. Helen wants to escape
        2. Sonya works

    IV. The future
        1. Helen rejects her one chance to be happy
        2. Sonya accepts lonely life

C. Conclusion

Point-form Outline

Once you have mapped out the substructure of the Skeleton Outline, you need to isolate the supporting details for your argument. This should not be a lengthy process because you have a structure in place, a clear idea of the direction your essay is taking, and a good overall knowledge of the contents of your notes. To include every detail unearthed during the research will overwhelm the reader and destroy the clarity of your answer; therefore, further selection is necessary. Read through your notes, carefully selecting only what is essential to your argument. Be ruthless and reject the irrelevant notes. The supporting details are arranged under the structure of the Basic and the Skeleton Outlines as shown on the following page. This stage is known as the Point-form Outline.

Remember that the purpose of your essay is to develop an answer or response to your research question and to articulate it in the form of an argument or thesis. You are not chronicling the life of Anton Chekhov or summarizing *Uncle Vanya* in our example. You are explaining the way in which **you think** the female characters shape the mood in *Uncle Vanya*.

Your judgments, interpretations, and opinions have to be supported by relevant evidence and developed through sound reasoning if your argument is to be credible and convincing. Your supporting evidence will come in the form of examples and quotations from primary texts and references to secondary sources, such as critical comments from literary scholars. To fashion a successful essay requires the fusing of your supporting evidence with insight, reason, and logic.

Your responsibility is to produce a reasoned response and a balanced presentation of your point of view. You must not "stack the deck" by consciously selecting material to promote a preconceived position. Your essay represents a delicate balance of emotional engagement and dispassionate distance indelibly stamped with your imprint. These philosophical considerations, already referred to on pages 58–59, are important in the practical process of constructing your Point-form Outline.

Use as few words as possible in the Point-form Outline; do not rewrite your notes. You can always refer to your research notes to check details when writing the rough draft. Since the order of the body sections may change during the drafting, it is advisable to devote a separate page of notepaper to each major section in the Point-form Outline, as shown below. It will be easy to rearrange the sections in the preferred order when preparing the rough draft.

We have taken section I of the body to illustrate the organization of the Point-form Outline.

Point-form Outline

B.I. Relationships with male characters

1. Tension increased by Helen's presence
   —Serebryakov's awareness that she is unhappy
   —Astrov and Vanya compete for Helen
   —Helen's rejection causes them both to despair
   —Helen resigned to loveless marriage

2. Sonya offers comfort
   —tries to help Astrov stop drinking
   —accepts Astrov's rejection
   —her life of self-sacrifice
   —tries to soothe Vanya

If you have been using a computer, look through your electronic notes, isolating the subsections of the Skeleton Outline and the supporting details of the Point-form Outline. Most word processors allow you to open more than one document window at a time, enabling you to develop your outline in one window while viewing your notes in the other. Most word processing programs also have an Outline function. This function will automatically number the sections and subsections as you go along, making it easy for you to create outlines.

Developing the three outlines is not excessively time-consuming. The outlines will enable you to determine if there are any weak spots in the argument. For instance, a Point-form Outline might show you that one of your main sections contains insufficient material to support your thesis, and that it might be better to merge it with another section or eliminate it. Furthermore, the outlines will expedite drafting your essay. "Writer's block" is rarely a problem if you are in control of your material **before** attempting to draft your essay.

Notice in the diagram below how the expansion of "B. I" is shown at each outline stage. Clarity of argument is a function of both style and structure. In shaping your outlines you will have created the structure. Style is the mortar that will hold the essay together and enhance clarity.

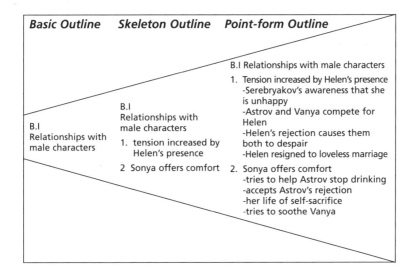

Basic Outline	Skeleton Outline	Point-form Outline
		B.I Relationships with male characters
		1. Tension increased by Helen's presence -Serebryakov's awareness that she is unhappy -Astrov and Vanya compete for Helen -Helen's rejection causes them both to despair -Helen resigned to loveless marriage
B.I Relationships with male characters	B.I Relationships with male characters 1. tension increased by Helen's presence 2 Sonya offers comfort	2. Sonya offers comfort -tries to help Astrov stop drinking -accepts Astrov's rejection -her life of self-sacrifice -tries to soothe Vanya

THE ROUGH DRAFT

Whether you are writing an essay on a single primary text or a research paper based on multiple sources, it is essential that you allow time in your schedule to prepare a rough draft. Roughing out the **complete** essay in a preliminary draft and laying it out in the required format will enhance the final copy significantly. If you use a computer to prepare your rough draft, producing the final copy will be a quick and painless process.

The presentation of your point of view must follow the standard conventions of essay writing; these conventions must be incorporated in your rough draft. Some are described in this section while others are explained later in the manual. **Before** commencing your rough draft, read through the items listed below, even though you may be conversant with some of them from writing essays based solely on primary texts. Although you may have discussed some of these items at the outset of the assignment, confirm your instructor's preferences before proceeding with the rough draft.

- Method of documentation

- Use of quotations

- Length

- Overall structure

- Opposing viewpoints

- Style and expression

- Paragraphing

- Appendix

- Title

- Table of contents

- Final copy format

Once you have completed the Point-form Outline, most of the hard work is over. If you have arranged the sections of the Point-form Outline on separate pages, it is now easy to rearrange them in a more appropriate order. Having worked extensively on the detailed outlines, you should have a clear idea of the relative importance of each section. Normally an ascending order of interest and importance is the most effective way of developing your thesis.

Once you have finalized the order of the main sections, the shape of your paper will have emerged. It is a relatively easy task to start fleshing the essay out and weaving it together in a rough draft now that you have a detailed structure in place. All the work that went into preparing the outlines will start to pay off. Another advantage is that the detailed outlines provide a formula for developing your paragraphs, as explained on pages 74–77. With your course clearly mapped out, a detailed structure in place and a clear grasp of the main features, your essay will progress under its own momentum.

One matter that you have to consider (and discuss with your instructor) is whether you should address arguments and ideas that run counter to your thesis, or whether you should ignore opposing viewpoints. It is not an issue if you are focusing solely on a primary text, but in longer research assignments, challenging counter arguments will lend an enhanced credibility to your thesis. Rebuttals should be inserted where they fit most naturally into the overall structure of the essay, and they must be included in planning the detailed outlines. You can refute contradictory viewpoints immediately after the thesis statement, or at appropriate places as you develop and substantiate your thesis. Alternatively, you may address other points of view in footnotes or endnotes.

How long should the essay be? This is one of the most common questions raised by students. In many cases your instructor will determine the length of the paper and you should never exceed that length by more than ten percent. If no word limit is set, the length will be established by the demands of the question and your response to it. Shorter rather than longer is a sound rule to follow. Remember that your words should be weighed, not counted.

If you are using a computer, you should again take advantage of the fact that most word processors allow you to work on two documents simultaneously, usually by splitting the screen into two windows as shown below. Bring up your outline in one window and begin writing the essay in the other window. You can switch back and forth easily. You can also bring up the files that serve as your electronic notes in one window and transfer relevant information into the window where you are writing the draft by cutting and pasting. Use this feature sparingly, however, because an essay constructed by mindlessly stringing together your research notes will not make any sense to your readers.

Once you have completed the rough draft you can work on the essay in fullscreen mode. You may find it useful to increase the line spacing and widen the margins when printing a draft copy so that you will have more white space for revising and editing. Do not forget to remove the extra space before printing the final copy.

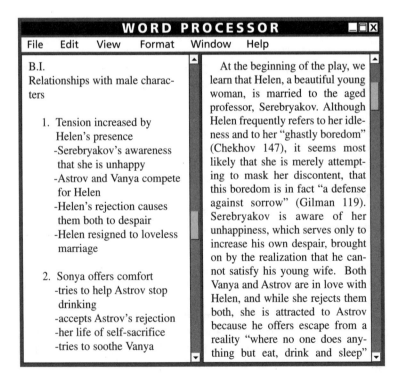

Drafting the Introduction

The introduction should prepare the reader by providing the background and by establishing the direction of the essay. Although usually short, introductions are important because they set the general tone of your work and because first impressions can influence the reader. Since essays and term papers are scholarly studies, it is inappropriate to inject humour and sensationalism into the introduction to "grab" the reader's attention. Try to "introduce" the reader to your essay in a more serious and formal, yet nevertheless interesting, manner. If you have followed a systematic research and outlining process, you should have no difficulty in drafting the introduction first. Do not leave the introduction until last, almost as an afterthought.

Introductions normally start with background information. This information, which is largely descriptive, narrative, or biographical in nature, provides the reader with a clear idea of the topic and the focus of the essay. **The key element of any introduction to an essay on a work of literature is an explicit statement of the thesis or argument** — it is the axis around which the essay revolves. It is important to inform the reader of your position or point of view before you start developing it in the body of your essay. Academic papers are not detective thrillers aimed at keeping the reader in suspense until the final paragraph.

Check with your instructor before using the first person in the thesis statement. Many instructors discourage the use of "I" in an essay. Check also the preferred length of the thesis statement with your instructor. Should it be a concise single sentence or a two-sentence assertion, or should it be an expanded explanation detailing the argument? Some instructors even recommend a description of the structure of the essay as part of an expanded thesis statement.

Despite its brevity, the introduction is an important and integral part of your essay. It will probably vary from about 10 to 15 percent of the overall length of the essay, but it must never overwhelm and overshadow the development of your argument in the body of the essay. No matter the length or the nature of the introduction, try to mention the three P's — the **problem**, the **purpose**, and your **point of view**.

The matter of the contents of an introduction is a contentious issue. Except for the need to state the thesis or argument, there is little consensus among instructors on structuring an introduction. Therefore, it is especially important to discuss the nature and the length of the introduction with your instructor prior to starting your essay.

The debate is focused primarily on whether it is necessary to indicate the precise objective of the essay to the reader by inserting either the question or, alternatively, a statement of purpose in the introduction. Some instructors believe that since the question directed the process of preparing the essay, and the thesis is the answer to that question, then the question explicitly expressed in the introduction is the clearest signpost to the reader of the intended direction of the essay.

On the other hand, many instructors believe that it is disruptive and artificial to insert a question or statement of purpose in the introduction. They argue that the combination of a concise title and a well-defined thesis offers adequate direction to the reader.

Below you will find a sample introduction to the essay on *Uncle Vanya* that includes just background information and a thesis statement. Other examples of extended introductions are presented in the pages ahead.

The plays of Anton Chekhov do not rely on dramatic staging or complicated plots. Instead, Chekhov employs a more subtle technique of focusing on the creation of an appropriate mood through which he compels the reader to participate in the experience of his characters.

Uncle Vanya provides a glimpse into a bleak and dispirited world, a world of resignation and defeat where human potential has been squandered. In Uncle Vanya the two female characters, Helen and Sonya, play a key role in shaping and sustaining the dark and sombre mood throughout the play. Their reaction to the male characters, to each other, and to their surroundings reinforces the play's feeling of quiet despair.

The funnel model offers a framework for a longer introduction.[5] The funnel formula moves through a series of steps, from general **background** information to a specific **statement of thesis.** The **focus** (problem or issue) of the essay requires explanation and its importance, either in relation to the primary text or as a field of study, should be clarified. Stating your research question is probably the clearest means of expressing the purpose of the essay. If you find it difficult to integrate a question smoothly into the text of the introduction, try stating the objective of the assignment in a more traditional way, such as "The purpose of this paper is to explain how the female characters shape the mood in *Uncle Vanya*." At all costs **avoid** phrasing the objective of the assignment as follows: "The purpose of this paper is to prove that . . ." Your purpose is not to prove — there is no final proof in literary studies — but to develop and substantiate an answer to the question in an impartial but convincing manner.

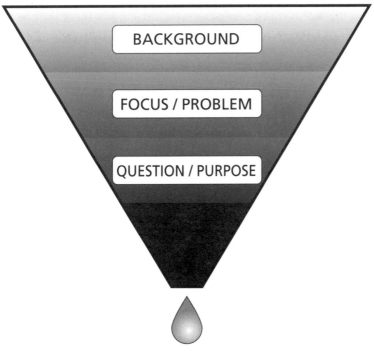

BACKGROUND

FOCUS / PROBLEM

QUESTION / PURPOSE

THESIS STATEMENT / POINT OF VIEW

Below you will find another introduction to the Chekhov essay based on the funnel formula described on the previous page. It is shown here in final form after revising and editing. We have used a subheading for illustrative purposes only; many instructors discourage subheadings, especially in shorter essays.

Introduction

The plays of Anton Chekhov explore issues such as the class system and the role of women in Russian society at the end of the 19th century. These issues remain relevant today, giving his work a universal quality that is still appreciated by modern readers. Chekhov's characters are finely rendered and while they may seem to belong to another era, readers can identify with their sorrows and their losses. Following the tradition of Russian drama, Chekhov does not rely on dramatic staging or complicated plots. Instead, he employs a more subtle technique, focusing on the creation of an appropriate mood, through which he compels the reader to participate in the experience of his characters.

In Uncle Vanya, Chekhov provides a glimpse into a sombre world, a world of resignation and defeat, in which human potential has been squandered and happiness eludes all. The play explores the wasted lives of the characters as they experience their own isolation and grief. The mood remains dark throughout the play, and while it seems that Chekhov intends the focus to be on Vanya, it is the female characters who play a key role in sustaining the mood as the story unfolds. This raises the question of how the female characters are so presented that they become vital elements in shaping the mood of the play.

The two female characters, Helen and Sonya, influence the dark and sombre mood of the play by the ways in which they relate to the significant male characters and to each other. Both their reaction to their surroundings and their placid resignation to the future further emphasize the play's feeling of quiet despair.

Like the outlines in the primary text and comparative essays, the detailed outlines offer a formula for developing your paragraphs. For a major research paper, however, the formula has to be expanded. The components of the funnel and the "coffee filter" shown below, which are simply the subsections of the Skeleton Outline introduction on page 62, provide the paragraph structure for the introduction. The Point-form Outline will supply the supporting details. Both the funnel and the filter are flexible models for paragraphing an introduction, and you will notice in the example on the previous page that we have combined the focus and the purpose in one paragraph.

If you are undertaking a major term paper based on a variety of primary and secondary sources, you may wish to indicate the range of viewpoints and the nature of the intellectual debate surrounding the focus of your research in the introduction. Simply add a base to the funnel (and another paragraph), converting it into a coffee filter as shown below.

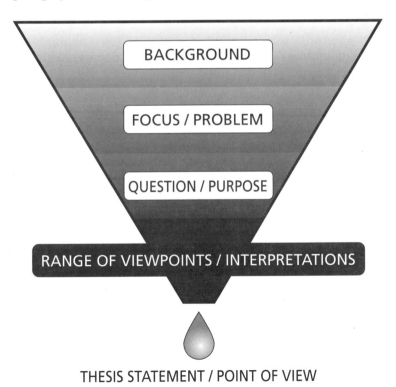

Drafting the Body

With a completed Point-form Outline, it is a relatively easy task to draft the body of your essay. As we have emphasized repeatedly, the outlines, in addition to ensuring structure and clarity, also shape the paragraphs. The formula for paragraphing a major research paper is merely an expansion of the method described for the primary text essay on page 14. On the previous page we explained how the outlines provide a flexible formula for creating the paragraph structure for an extended introduction.

Below we have reproduced "B.I Relationships with the male characters" from page 64 to illustrate how the sub-sections of the Skeleton Outline provide the paragraph structure for the body of a major essay, while the details of the Point-form Outline supply the supporting evidence for each paragraph. The transformation of "B.I" from outline to paragraphed copy is shown on the following pages. Note that **only a single section** of the body is shown here because space precludes reproducing the whole essay.

This formula is not a rigid prescription for paragraphing; the detailed outlines simply provide a guide to developing a clear, coherent system. Some organizing scheme is essential because paragraphing remains one of the major difficulties encountered by students.

B.I. Relationships with male characters	**(introductory paragraph)**
1.Tension increased by Helen's presence	**(paragraph)**
-Serebryakov's awareness that she is unhappy -Astrov and Vanya compete for Helen -Helen's rejection causes them both to despair -Helen resigned to loveless marriage	
2.Sonya offers comfort	**(paragraph)**
-tries to help Astrov stop drinking -accepts Astrov's rejection -her life of self-sacrifice -tries to soothe Vanya	
	(concluding paragraph)

Much of the influence that the female characters exert on the mood of the play stems from their relationships with the male characters, all of whom are in a state of despair. Helen's relationships with Serebryakov, Vanya, and Astrov seem to increase the tension and darken the mood. Sonya attempts to offer comfort to the three men, and yet she is unable to draw them out of their misery, which casts another shadow over the characters. Although she too must eventually resign herself to her own sorrow, she does not entirely succumb to the despairing atmosphere; rather, she attempts to bring a state of calm to the household.

At the beginning of the play, we learn that Helen, a beautiful young woman, is married to the aged professor, Serebryakov. Although Helen frequently refers to her idleness and to her "ghastly boredom" (Chekhov 147), it seems most likely that she is merely attempting to mask her discontent, that this boredom is in fact "a defense against sorrow" (Gilman 119). Serebryakov is aware of her unhappiness, which serves only to increase his own despair, brought on by the realization that he cannot satisfy his young wife. Both Vanya and Astrov are in love with Helen, and while she rejects them both, she is attracted to Astrov because he offers escape from a reality "where no one does anything but eat, drink and sleep" (Chekhov 147). Although she longs "to fall under the spell of such a man, to forget everything" (Chekhov 147), Helen barely acknowledges her attraction to Astrov, and refuses to act on it, even though she has the chance of achieving happiness with him. Helen's dismissal of Vanya's advances causes Vanya even more bitterness and regret than he already feels. The rivalry between Astrov and Vanya for Helen's affections causes tensions to mount, and her rejection of both men results in a melancholic atmosphere that pervades each remaining scene.

While it appears that Helen's presence causes tension among the men, Sonya's presence seems to bring a brief calm to the emotionally turbulent atmosphere. Her name, signifying "wisdom" (Meister 242), reflects her gentle nature. She convinces Astrov to stop drinking for several hours by using his own philosophy: "You're always saying that man doesn't create anything, that he only destroys what God has given him. Then why, oh why, destroy your own self?" (Chekhov 139). Unlike Helen, who ignites the male characters' hopes of finding some solace in her love, only to thoroughly dampen their hopes, Sonya attempts to comfort them. Ironically, Sonya's dream of finding some affection and solace from Astrov only results in her rejection by him so that she, too, must resign herself to a life of solitude. Despite her sense of loss, she is still able to offer consolation to Vanya, who appears to have completely surrendered to his anguish by the end of the play. While the mood is still sombre, the strength of her conviction seems to bring a momentary calm. In the final moment of Act Four, she looks beyond her own sadness to reach out to him:

> *We shall find peace. We shall hear the angels, we shall see the sky sparkling with diamonds. We shall see all the evils of this life, all our own sufferings, vanish in the flood of mercy which will fill the whole world [. . .] I believe that, I do believe it. [. . .] We shall find peace. (Chekhov 167)*

While there is a hint of optimism in this speech, Sonya's words to Vanya do in fact maintain the dark tone of the play, as her optimism is ultimately muted by her closing words which suggest desperately-willed belief.

Helen's cold response to Vanya and then to Astrov's romantic overtones underlines the emotional inertia that pervades the play. Sonya's futile endeavours to offer Vanya some consolation and to encourage Astrov to improve himself strike a flat note and, ironically, the serenity that she exudes intensifies the sombre mood of despair.

You will notice from the previous example that each major section of the body follows a miniature ABC structure. An introductory paragraph introduces the section, "body" paragraphs develop the main point ("relationships with the male characters"), and a concluding paragraph sums up the section. The ABC formula also operates at the individual paragraph level. A topic sentence clearly states the main idea, followed by sentences that provide supporting detail. A concluding sentence sums up the paragraph and clarifies its role in the development of your thesis and may also act as a transition to the next paragraph.

Paragraphs are like links in a chain. Just as a chain is only as strong as its weakest link, so is your essay only as effective as its weakest paragraph. Give unity and cohesion to your paragraphs by eliminating what is irrelevant to the main idea or focal point of each paragraph. Subheadings tend to fragment the unity of an essay. **With proper paragraphing, there is no need for subheadings in an essay**. Paragraphs with a central focus, explicit topic sentences, and suitable transitional words provide the unity, flow, and signposts that prevent the reader from getting lost in a maze of words. The clarity of your argument is largely a function of the structure of your material and the style of its presentation. Paragraphs provide the bridging between style and structure, and significantly enhance clarity.

The body of the essay is the most important section and the longest. It is devoted entirely to the development and substantiation of the thesis that was stated at the end of the introduction — that is **the sole function of the body of the essay.** Successful essays have the focus and clarity of a laser beam, not the chaotic brilliance of a fireworks display. Give your essay focus and clarity by explicitly linking all the ideas and information to your thesis and anchoring your argument in relevant evidence and examples. Instructors look for incisive analysis and argument, not for summaries of plots, aimless descriptions of characters, or thoughtless regurgitation of critical sources.

Remember that your chief responsibility is to construct and advance a systematic, logical, and convincing thesis — one that is carefully structured, convincingly argued, substantiated with evidence, and clearly expressed.

Drafting the Conclusion

In the final section you weave together the various threads of the thesis and sum up the supporting points. The conclusion should not be a dull summary of the major sections but a subtle linking of the main ideas that you developed in the body. Do not add new information in the conclusion to support your thesis; if the information is important, it should be included in the body of the essay, and not added as an afterthought to the conclusion. Also, ensure that any quotations have a specific function, and that they are not simply inserted in the conclusion for dramatic effect. Your conclusion might benefit from a comment on how your thesis fits into a wider literary context or a suggestion of further questions and ideas for exploration. The conclusion is brief, usually one paragraph, but it is important because it is the last opportunity to impress the reader with the validity of your arguments. Remember that last impressions are usually lasting impressions. Below you will find the conclusion of the Chekhov essay.

The female characters play a pivotal role in the creation of the sombre mood that exists throughout Uncle Vanya. *It is through their relationships with other characters, through their reaction to their surroundings, and through their acceptance of a life without change that such a mood is sustained. By crafting the female characters so that they continually influence the atmosphere, Chekhov is able to bring a depth of feeling and meaning to the drama that the more stylized devices of plot and staging could not have achieved. There is a tragedy within this play, but "it is not brought about by grand events, by major forces of evil: it results from the trivial and petty unpleasantnesses of day-to-day living" (Peace 74).* Uncle Vanya *is a poignant play, not because it relates the story of the downfall of tyrants or recounts a mythological adventure, but because it presents complex characters dealing with pain that we recognize, and consequently, we are actively and intimately engaged in Chekhov's work.*

Table of Contents

A contents page provides the reader with an outline of the structure of your essay and lists supplementary features, such as the documentation system and the appendix. The contents page follows the title page and the abstract (if used). The letters of the alphabet in our example below correspond to the organization used throughout the research and outlining stages. Avoid using the term "Body" in your table of contents. It was used in the research and in the outlines to assist you in understanding the structure of an essay. Short essays seldom require a table of contents, and some instructors do not even insist on a contents page for longer papers. Consult your instructor about the requirements for the table of contents. There is usually no need to include page references, unless you are writing a dissertation or a major paper.

Contents

A. Introduction

B. I. Relationships with
       Male Characters
   II. Relationships with
        Female Characters
   III. Reaction to the Surroundings
   IV. The Future

C. Conclusion

D. Appendix

E. Works Consulted

Title Page

The instructor sees your title page first; therefore, ensure that it clearly and concisely indicates the focus of your essay and that it is clearly and neatly laid out. We have not repeated the layout of the title page; for details, refer to page 16. The title of the Chekhov essay could be phrased as follows:

**Shaping the Mood in *Uncle Vanya:*
The Role of the Female Characters**

Illustrations

There are two major types of illustrations: tables and figures. Tables contain columns of statistical data. Figures consist of photographs, maps, drawings, graphs, diagrams, charts, and pictures. Illustrations are used less frequently in literature essays than in social studies assignments. Check with your instructor whether illustrations should be included. If you use illustrations, select them judiciously and always ask yourself whether each figure actually illustrates a point in your essay. As with textual evidence, your criterion must always be: is an illustration relevant to your thesis or point of view? If you plan to use an illustration, such as a genealogical chart to show family relationships, check with your instructor whether it should be included in the text or placed in the appendix.

Appendix

The appendix is a useful place at the end of your essay for important information that is too extensive to be placed in the body. The material must be relevant to the thesis of your paper and must be cross-referenced in either a footnote or a parenthetical reference. Guard against the temptation to pack the appendix with unnecessary material. An appendix to an English essay might include, for example, a chronological listing of all the published works of a writer. The appendix is placed before the endnotes (if used) and the bibliography, and each section is numbered and titled. See pages 121–151 of this manual for an example.

Documentation

Ensure that you have used a style of documentation that is appropriate to writing literary essays and also conforms to your instructor's requirements. Read the documentation section (pages 93–112) carefully because the citations and the list of sources have to be included in your rough draft. A sample list of sources for the Chekhov essay based on the MLA style is provided on page 110.

The Abstract

If you plan to provide an abstract (a short synopsis of the essay), refer to page 132 in the Appendix for details and then rough it out in the preliminary draft.

Check the requirements regarding the format of the final copy with your instructor and then ensure that you have incorporated **all the sections and features** of your essay in the rough draft. Revising, editing, and preparing the final copy (which are all covered in the following pages) will be much easier and quicker if you have roughed out the **complete** essay. In addition to following the standard conventions of essay writing, your essay will also be assessed according to standard criteria. Therefore, review the criteria and then review your draft to ensure that it conforms to all the criteria against which the essay will be assessed.

REVISING AND EDITING

Once you have completed your rough draft, you are ready to start revising and editing. The clarity of the argument you are developing and presenting is determined largely by the structure of your answer and the style of your expression. Revising involves reviewing the draft for structure and organization. Editing involves refining the style and expression of the revised draft. These are important stages for preparing a quality essay, and you must allow time in your schedule for revising and editing.

Set the draft aside for a few days before starting to revise it. Getting a little "distance" allows you to reflect on it and will sharpen your eye considerably. If you based your rough draft on a Point-form Outline, you will reduce the amount of revising substantially. The extra work that went into the preparation and planning invariably pays off in the long run.

Your first task is to examine the order of the main sections of the body. Although you may have rearranged the sections at the Point-form Outline stage, the order might appear disjointed in the rough draft. Whether you place your most important section first or last will be determined by the argument. The question to ask yourself is whether there is a smooth, logical flow in the sequence of the sections. Check the introduction to make sure that the problem, the purpose and your point of view are clearly spelled out. Does the conclusion sum up the main points of the argument and provide an effective culmination to the essay?

Once you are satisfied with the overall structure, look closely at the paragraphing. Identify the topic sentence in each paragraph to ensure that there is a central focal point. Is there sufficient supporting detail in each paragraph? Is there unity to each paragraph? Are all topic sentences linked to the thesis? Is there a natural flow in the sequence of the paragraphs? Is there any repetitious or contradictory information? Are there any vague and general observations? Do the quotations fit? These are the types of questions you should ask yourself as you revise the rough draft. But above all, ask yourself whether the essay develops and delivers a clear and convincing point of view.

If you have made many changes, it may be necessary to rewrite a handwritten draft. Revising a word-processed draft is much easier. Revising and rewriting drafts is not wasted time, because the quality of the essay will improve with each draft. Prominent writers repeatedly emphasize the importance of revising and editing. William Zinsser points out that "rewriting is the essence of writing well"[6] and Strunk and White stress that "revising is part of writing."[7]

Since editing is largely concerned with fine-tuning and polishing your language and expression, you should reread the section on Style. It is a good practice to have a thesaurus, a dictionary, a manual of style, and a guide to discriminatory language at hand when you are editing your draft. Read through your revised draft slowly, concentrating carefully on the text as you edit.

- Are the spelling and grammar correct?

- Does the punctuation improve the flow of the essay?

- Have you chosen your words carefully?

- Have you eliminated unnecessary words and phrases?

- Is your draft free of discriminatory language?

- Can you vary the structure and length of sentences?

- Is capitalization consistent?

- Can you substitute active for passive verbs?

- Are the verb tenses consistent?

- Have you eliminated contractions?

The next step is to read your draft aloud. You can read it to yourself or tape record it. You may read it to someone else or perhaps have that person read it while you listen. If it is difficult to read and sounds stilted, edit the draft until it flows smoothly and naturally. Ask a friend to review the draft, because an independent critic will often detect flaws that pass unnoticed by the writer. Once the editing is complete, read the essay aloud another time. An essay that "speaks well" is invariably an essay that reads well. By eliminating "static" and giving your essay rhythm and resonance, you can dramatically enhance the impact of the message.[8]

The word processor is an invaluable writing tool. It can speed up the revising and editing process, and enhance the quality of your assignments. The advantage of word processing is that once the information is typed, revision and editing can be done without rewriting and retyping the draft. But it is essential to do the preliminary structuring, outlining, and drafting. A word processor has more important uses than simply cutting and pasting paragraphs in a disorganized piece of writing.

It is not always easy to get a feel for the overall structure of an essay on a computer monitor, nor is it easy to detect punctuation or spelling errors. You should revise and edit on a printed copy of the draft as well as on the screen. Using the draft function, you can triple-space your copy and also create wider margins to make space for corrections and comments. Another advantage of a printed copy is that it is easier to read aloud. It can also be read and checked by others. You can then make the changes on the screen and print another copy for further editing.

If you are revising and editing on a computer, you may wish to keep all your electronic drafts. In this case simply name each revision, such as "Vanya1" and "Vanya2" and so on. This will allow you to return to earlier versions for material that you deleted in later revisions. After you have produced your final copy, you can erase the earlier files. Alternatively, you could keep printed copies of earlier versions.

Whether you are printing copies or editing on the screen, it is important that you frequently **save your draft** on both the hard drive and on a floppy disk to avoid losing your essay if there is a power failure or your hard drive malfunctions. Instructors no longer accept the excuse of a "computer crash." Also unacceptable is the excuse that the essay could not be printed because the printer ran out of ink or paper.

If your word processor has a spell check, a thesaurus or a grammar check program, take advantage of it when you are editing. It will often find errors and provide useful suggestions, but it cannot provide a guarantee for the quality of your essay. Some software may not be able to detect the difference between "to," "too," and "two" or between "cite," "sight," and "site." It remains your responsibility to edit your work carefully, regardless of the software you use.

THE FINAL COPY

Leave yourself enough time in your schedule to set aside your edited draft for a few days before you prepare the final copy. Producing the final copy is simply finalizing the edited draft — it is the final tuning of the essay. If you have followed a systematic process of researching, outlining, drafting, revising, and editing, preparing the final copy should be quick and painless, especially if you use a word processor. Converting the rough draft to the final copy is the real test of the advice repeated throughout the manual: **the more time and effort you expend initially, the less is needed at the end.**

Your completed essay is the product of a lengthy and intensive process. Much of the process never appears in the final copy, but the process is nevertheless essential to the quality of the final copy.* Although the process — in the form of notes, outlines, and drafts — is sometimes evaluated, frequently instructors will base their assessment solely on the essay that is submitted — the one tenth of the iceberg above the water. If one tenth counts for 100 percent of the mark, then it is especially important that you package the final copy with painstaking care.

Computer technology will enhance the appearance of your essay. Software programs facilitate attractive layout of text and illustrations, and modern printers support a variety of font styles and ensure a clean, professional type. Most schools and universities have computer facilities that are accessible to students, so there is no need to purchase expensive equipment. Combining literary ability with typing and computing skills is an important asset today. Remember, however, that it is substance that characterizes a good essay. Technological dazzle alone is insufficient.

Individual instructors sometimes have their own preferences with regard to format, so it is advisable to check manuscript requirements again before starting the final copy. If your instructor has expressed no specific preference, consider formatting your essay as outlined on the next page.

---

* Keep your notes, outlines, and drafts: they are your best defence against a charge of plagiarism. Always keep a backup copy of your essay as well in case the original is lost.

- Use standard-sized white unlined paper.

- Type double-space on one side of the page only.

- Use a common font like Times New Roman and a standard font size, usually 12 point.

- Leave at least a 2.5 cm or 1-inch margin all the way around the page.

- Number pages accurately.

- Avoid section headings, as they tend to disrupt the argument.

- If headings are used, ensure that they are consistent in style and size.

- Do not leave white spaces between the introduction and the body and between the body and the conclusion. Your paragraphs should act as signposts to the reader.

- A "ragged" right margin is recommended because the text is easier to read than with full justified margins, which can create uneven spacing.

- Do not staple the pages together if you are using endnotes, because some instructors like to remove the endnotes and refer to them as they read the essay. Consider using a paperclip instead or placing your essay in a folder.

- Cover folders are required by some instructors, but discouraged by others.

- If in doubt about manuscript requirements, always consult your instructor.

Proofread your essay meticulously from title page to bibliography. You might ask a friend to do a second proofreading. Frequent errors create a poor impression and will have a negative effect on the evaluation of the essay. On the other hand, an error-free and attractively laid-out essay will make a positive impact on the reader. The extra time devoted to revising, editing, and proofreading your essay is well worth it. There is a close relationship between effort and quality, and a good piece of work will always reflect the time and care taken in its preparation.

QUOTATIONS

In writing about literature, you are dealing with the written word, whether you are focusing on a single primary text or using secondary critical sources for a research paper. Unlike many other disciplines that rely on empirical data, such as statistics and graphs, your "data" is the written word. As you analyze, interpret, and draw conclusions from literary material, you will need to refer to it either directly or indirectly in order to illustrate and reinforce your interpretations and arguments. You will have to decide when to use paraphrased ideas and information and when to quote directly from the source material. Quotations, from either primary or secondary sources, can be effectively used in the following situations:

- As evidence to illustrate and provide credibility for your arguments.

- To add authority to your point of view.

- To lend elegance and eloquence to your writing.

- To quote the author's central argument when challenging an opposing viewpoint.

- Where the original words better express the meaning than is possible by paraphrasing.

A cardinal rule in writing essays and papers is: **Do not overquote.** Parachuting quotations into the essay simply as space-fillers or for dramatic effect will destroy the clarity of the essay. Also avoid name-dropping of literary authorities simply for effect. Comments from authorities may indicate the breadth and depth of your research but "to indulge yourself too often in the quoting of others' great thoughts is to run the risk of never learning to formulate your own."[9] It is your interpretations and ideas that the instructor wants to read.

Quotations alone do not constitute indisputable evidence, nor do they speak for themselves. Therefore, quotations must be firmly anchored in the text of your essay and explicitly linked to the thesis. Do not just dangle quotations in front of your reader; introduce each quotation by identifying the work or author, place it in context, and explain it. It is the strength of your arguments that will finally convince the reader of the validity of your thesis. Does each quotation serve a purpose? If not, eliminate it.

Not only should you select your quotations carefully, but you should keep them short. If you decide to quote a primary excerpt or a secondary expert, select only the essential words and use ellipses (. . .) as shown on the following pages. Remember that clarity of argument is your key objective. Cluttering your essay with lengthy quotations — no matter how relevant — does not promote clarity.

Integrating your quotations smoothly into the text of the essay can enhance clarity. Short quotations of less than forty words or less than four lines should be merged as naturally as possible into the text of the essay and enclosed within quotation marks, as shown below.

Alice Munro's impeccable technique, her "postmodern view of language," is one reason for the international interest in her fiction.

Longer quotations of more than forty words or four lines should be separated from the text as shown in the example on the next page. The quoted passage (also known as a block quotation) starts on a new line and is usually introduced with a colon. Quotation marks are omitted. A block quotation is indented between four and ten spaces from the left margin, depending on the preferences of your instructor or on the recommendation of the manual you are using. The Modern Language Association (MLA) recommends a ten-space indention, while *A Manual for Writers* by Kate Turabian suggests four spaces. For simplicity and convenience, it may be easier to use either one or two tab stops for indenting block quotations. Once again, there is no consensus on spacing block quotations. MLA recommends double-spacing and *A Manual for Writers* suggests single-spacing. Check spacing requirements with your instructor if you are uncertain. Illustrated below is an example of a block quotation.

Beryl's version of the event is substantially different than the version Fame has heard from her mother. Fame ponders:

> **Why shouldn't Beryl's version of the same event be different from my mother's? Beryl was strange in every way — everything about her was slanted, seen from a new angle. It was my mother's version that held, for a time [. . .]. But Beryl's story didn't vanish; it stayed sealed-off for years but it wasn't gone.**

There are no rigid rules for quoting, merely guidelines. You may wish to deviate from the suggestions above to improve the meaning or the layout of the essay. For example, you may decide that it is more effective to separate a short quotation of two sentences in a block quotation rather than try to merge it in the text of the essay.

If it is necessary to omit part of a quotation because of length or irrelevance, use three spaced periods (. . .) enclosed in square brackets, as shown in the previous example. This is known as an ellipsis. However, you must not alter the meaning of the passage or make it incomprehensible through your own omission of words. You must also ensure that the modified quotation is grammatically correct.

If you are quoting material between one and three lines long from a poem or a play, incorporate the excerpt in the text of the essay, enclosing it in quotation marks. Lines are separated by a slash, as shown below.

In his final soliloquy, Hamlet expresses his determination to act with vigour and resolve: "O! from this time forth, / My thoughts be bloody, or be nothing worth!"

Quotations of more than three lines from poems or plays are separated from the text and usually introduced with a colon. For plays, indent the quoted material one or two tab stops, using the exact layout of the excerpt, and omit quotation marks. Poems are usually centered on the page, as shown in the Wordsworth example below. *The MLA Handbook* recommends double-spacing for long quotations, while *A Manual for Writers* permits both single or double-spacing when separating excerpts from poems and plays in block quotations. Where a line or more of poetry is omitted from a block quotation, use a line of spaced periods the length of the line above. Enclose the extended ellipsis in square brackets as shown in the example below.

In "The Prelude," William Wordsworth emphasizes the restorative value of childhood experiences and memories:

Such moments
Are scattered everywhere, taking their date
From our first childhood: I remember well,
[. . . . .]
I am lost, but see
In simple childhood something of the base
On which thy greatness stands [. . .].

It is sometimes necessary to insert a word or phrase in a quotation for clarification or correction. If you have to insert words in a quotation to clarify its meaning, enclose them in square brackets.

"It seems so much the truth it is the truth; it's what I believe about them [her parents]. I haven't stopped believing it."

"The role [of the narrator] is to guide the reader through the complexities of the story."

If an error is present in the quoted material, use the Latin word "sic" (meaning "so" or "thus") to indicate the error. If "sic" is placed within the quotation, enclose it in square brackets, and if "sic" falls outside the quotation, then enclose it in parentheses, as demonstrated below.

McGregor's journal entry for the fifteenth of December contains the following cryptic comment on the relationship: "Lunched with Ian McTavish; he is still angery [sic] about the delay."

Arnold insists "You must have a disinterested atitude" (sic).

Single quotation marks are used where a quotation occurs within quoted material, as shown below. In a block quotation, where opening and closing quotation marks are omitted, any additional quoted material is enclosed in double quotation marks.

"Noble wrote in his diary that he had been subjected to 'cruel and unusual punishment' during his confinement."

Generally, punctuation marks such as commas and periods are placed within the quotation marks, while colons, semicolons, question marks, and exclamation marks go outside the quotation marks. However, any punctuation mark that is part of the quoted material is included within the quotation marks.

Do not burden the text with excessively long quotations over seven or ten lines long; they should be placed in the appendix and referred to in a note or a parenthetical reference. Always ask yourself whether a long quotation is essential or whether you could shorten it by the use of ellipses, or even eliminate it.

There are several ways you can distance yourself from quotations or ideas that are discriminatory. You can paraphrase the remark, replace the discriminatory words with bracketed substitutes, or use only the non-offensive words. If you need to quote in full, then use "(sic)" to indicate the inappropriate words.[10]

It is essential that you quote the material, including punctuation, accurately. To alter the wording or meaning of a quotation or to use a quotation out of context is unethical. Therefore, it is important that you transcribe quotations carefully during the analysis and recording.

To use the writing and ideas of other authors without acknowledgment is not only unethical, but illegal. There are procedures for acknowledging your sources so that you avoid charges of plagiarism. These citation procedures have been omitted from the quotation examples above to avoid confusion. They are explained in detail in the next section on Documentation.

The most common conventions for quoting have been covered in this section. For more complex forms, students should consult the *MLA Handbook, A Manual for Writers,* or their instructor. Above all, be consistent in the method you use for quoting.

Finally, remember to use quotations sparingly and judiciously. Consider whether paraphrasing or summarizing a point might be more effective than quoting it. A paper comprising numerous quotations strung together like a patchwork quilt is not an essay.

DOCUMENTATION

Introduction

It is essential that you identify and acknowledge the sources of information and ideas that you have used to develop and substantiate your arguments. Not only must direct quotations be documented, but paraphrased ideas and important factual details that you have borrowed from other writers must also be acknowledged.

Plagiarism is the unacknowledged use of someone else's ideas: it is a serious academic offence. Just as ignorance of the law is no excuse, there is no excuse for "accidental" plagiarism. Careful documentation will help you avoid charges of plagiarism. Since each of your notes was coded with a source and page reference, it is easy to identify and acknowledge all important details and ideas in your essay.

Factual information that is common knowledge need not be documented. For instance, you do not have to document a source stating that William Shakespeare was born in Stratford-on-Avon. Frequently, determining what is common knowledge is not easy, but your judgment will improve with experience and practice. "Document when in doubt" is a safe route to follow, but do not overdo the use of citations. It is a mistake to attempt to impress the reader with reams of footnotes or parenthetical citations. Likewise, a lengthy list of sources in the bibliography, instead of inspiring awe, may arouse suspicion. Be guided by common sense as well as ethics when documenting your sources.[11]

Two key elements are used in documentation: the citation and the list of sources.

- The **citation** is a brief reference in the text of the essay identifying the source of the information, idea or quotation. Either a parenthetical (bracketed) reference or a number is used.

- The **list of sources** is placed at the end of the essay and provides details of the in-text citations and may include other sources used to prepare the assignment.

Two major documentation or citation systems (or styles) are used in literature, language and the humanities: the parenthetical author-page system and the numbered footnote/endnote system.

- **Author-Page:** The source is indicated by providing the author's last name and page reference in a parenthetical citation in the text of the essay. The reader can then refer to an alphabetical list of sources at the end of the essay to obtain complete bibliographic details. This method is described in the *MLA Handbook for Writers of Research Papers* published by the Modern Language Association of America (MLA).

- **Footnotes/Endnotes:** The source is indicated by using a superscript number in the text, which corresponds to an entry in a footnote or an endnote containing complete bibliographic details. These details are repeated in a slightly different order in a list of sources at the end of the essay. This method is described in *The Chicago Manual of Style, A Manual for Writers of Term Papers, Theses and Dissertations*, and the *MLA Handbook*.

Documenting your sources can serve a number of functions:

- The information and its context can be checked for accuracy.

- Other writers get credit for their ideas.

- Basing your research on sound scholarship will enhance its credibility.

- Readers are guided to additional sources of information on the topic.

The parenthetical author-page system (or "MLA style" as it is usually known) is widely used in writing about language and literature. The numbered footnote/endnote system, although still used in many humanities subjects, is used less frequently in language and literature. Consequently, we have devoted this chapter to a detailed explanation of the parenthetical MLA style of documentation.

The numbered endnote system, based on the Chicago/ Turabian style, has been used to document *The English Essay,* and the fundamentals of this system will be apparent in reading this manual. Students requiring a more detailed explanation of the numbered note system, illustrated with examples, should consult a companion manual, entitled *The Research Essay.*

Always check with your instructor to determine the preferred method of documentation for each essay. Remember, whichever method you choose, make sure that you follow the method consistently throughout your essay. And finally, strive for accuracy, simplicity, and clarity when documenting your sources.

Electronic resources are expanding at a remarkable rate. These sources can be divided into two main groups:

- Portable databases, such as CD-ROMs, which may be shared via a network.

- Online material available on the Internet and accessible by a computer, a modem and a browser through a service provider such as *America Online* or *Sympatico.* Online information is also available, usually for a fee, from services such as *Dialog,* and *InfoGlobe,* either by dial-up access or through the Internet.

Like traditional sources used in an essay, electronic sources must also be documented. Documenting portable databases, such as CD-ROMs, is not that different from documenting other types of sources. However, documentation procedures for online sources are considerably more complex, and a separate section (pages 106–109) has been devoted to these procedures. The nature and evaluation of electronic sources is covered under "Sources" in the Appendix.

Citing Sources

MLA recommends identifying and acknowledging the source of information by providing the author's last name and page number in a parenthetical citation in the text of the essay as follows:

Woolf's short stories and essays are her "most impressive accomplishment" (Steele 3).

The reader can then refer to the list of sources at the end of the essay to obtain complete bibliographic details. In the list of sources, the reference would be entered as follows:

Steele, Elizabeth. *Virginia Woolf's Literary Sources and Illusions.* New York: Garland, 1983.

The in-text procedure enables the reader to determine the sources quickly, but frequent parenthetical citations tend to disrupt the fluency of the text. Include just the essential citations. Improve readability by placing the citation at the end of a sentence or where a pause occurs, such as a punctuation mark, and include the author's name in the text if possible, as shown below.

As John Bailey, another Whitman biographer and critic, wrote in 1926, "All true poets live in the universal" (180).

Some of the more common forms of parenthetical citations are shown on the next two pages. Only the parenthetical citations are provided here; corresponding entries in the list of sources at the end of the essay are shown separately on pages 99–105.

Citing an entire work:

Charles Dickens' *Hard Times* is a novel of social realism.

Citing part of a work:

In *Timebends*, Arthur Miller describes his confrontations with the House Un-American Activities Committee (328-35, 357).

Citing a multivolume work:

Strindberg's complex dramatic structure is perfectly expressive of another key expressionistic idea: the illusory quality of time and space (Gassner 2: 780).

Citing a work listed by title:

The Oxford Companion to English Literature notes that W.H. Mallock is best known as the author of *The New Republic* (489).

Citing a work by a corporate author:

The Canadian Women's Indexing Group provides a retrospective index to 15 selected English and French-Canadian feminist periodicals (130).

Citing multiple works by the same author:

Lewis suggests that the textbook teaches "precisely nothing" about what it purports to teach *(Abolition of Man 5)*.

Citing indirect sources:

His description of himself in 1882 as "a young man of a very revolutionary and contradictory temperament" (qtd. in Shaw and Weintraub 114) reveals the essence of his complex personality.

Citing a play:

In his final soliloquy, Hamlet expresses his determination to act with vigour and resolve: "O! from this time forth, / My thoughts be bloody, or be nothing worth!" (*Hamlet* 4.4. 65–66)

Citing a poem:

In "Easter Wings," George Herbert uses line-length to shape his poem in a way that reflects the wasting power of sin on the narrator:

> My tender age in sorrow did begin:
> And still with sickness and shame
> Thou didst so punish sin
> That I became
> Most thin. (11-15)

Citing two works:

In Thomas Hardy's novels there is a strong sense of the inevitability of character and environment in the working out of human destiny (Grimsditch 28; Abercrombie 40).

Citing a work by two authors:

Strunk and White recommend avoiding the use of qualifiers (73).

Citing a source with multiple authors:

Literary criticism has historically been a much more retrograde activity than the imaginative writing it studies (Stephens et al. 224).

Listing Sources

Brief in-text parenthetical citations have to be linked to a detailed list of sources at the end of the essay. The citation "(Steele 3)" in the example below indicates to the readers that the information is drawn from page 3 of a work by Steele.

Woolf's short stories are her "most impressive accomplishment" (Steele 3).

In the list of sources at the end of the essay, readers will find the details of the work by Steele entered as follows:

Steele, Elizabeth. *Virginia Woolf's Literary Sources and Illusions.* New York: Garland, 1983.

Some instructors may only require a list of sources with details of the works cited in the essay. A list of cited sources is usually titled "Works Cited," although alternative terms such as "Sources Cited" or "Literature Cited" are usually acceptable. On the other hand, you may be asked to provide a list of all the sources that proved useful in preparing the essay, even if you did not cite all of them directly. If you included both useful sources and cited sources, you may use one of the following designations: "Works Consulted," "Bibliography," "Sources," "References," "Sources Consulted" or "List of Sources." **Always clarify the nature of the list of sources with your instructor.**

"Bibliography" is still a widely used term, but some instructors object to it on two counts. First, the word "bibliography" literally means a "list of books," and sources today range from books to interviews to databases. Secondly, "bibliography" implies a complete list of sources on a topic, and student sources for an essay are unlikely to represent an exhaustive list. Consider using "Select Bibliography" as an alternative designation.

Whatever procedure you choose, your sources should be listed in alphabetical order by author's last name in a separate section at the end of the essay. **Do not number your sources.** Most high school and university essays will require a single list of sources. For longer research papers and dissertations you may be required to classify your sources into primary and secondary material, published and unpublished information, or cited sources and additional sources. The classified structure of the Working Bibliography recommended earlier in this guide suggested that sources be grouped under headings, such as "Books," "Articles," and "Audio-Visual." This division was to encourage a diversity of sources. The final list of sources should not be grouped in this manner.

The entry for each source starts at the left margin with the author's last name listed first, followed by the initials or first name. If the entry extends beyond one line, the second and subsequent lines are indented five spaces or one tab space. Double-spacing is used between each line of an entry and also between individual entries. If there is no place of publication given, use "N.p." and for no publisher use "n.p." If both are missing, it is permissible to use just "N.p." If no date is provided for the source, insert "n.d." Abbreviations can be used for publishers, such as "Oxford UP" for "Oxford University Press."

You may be required to make descriptive or critical comments on the merits of each source, as shown below. In such a case, head your list of sources either "Annotated Bibliography" or "Annotated List of Works Cited" depending on the nature of the source list.

Livesay, Dorothy. *Right Hand, Left Hand.* Erin, ON: Press Porcepic, 1977.

This is Livesay's account of her life in Paris, Toronto, Montreal, and Vancouver in the 1930s. It is most useful for an understanding of the political radicalization of her poetry.

Shown on the following pages are examples of how to list the more common types of sources. These samples are based largely on the procedures described in the *MLA Handbook.* Students are advised to consult the manual for further details and more specialized forms.

BOOK

One Author

Michaels, Anne. *Fugitive Pieces.* Toronto: McClelland and Stewart, 1996.

Two or Three Authors

Howard, V.A., and J.H. Barton. *Thinking on Paper.* New York: Morrow, 1986.

More than Three Authors

Kaus, Carl, et al. *Stages of Drama.* Glenview: Scott, 1981.

Editor/Compiler

Howes, Barbara, ed. *Eye of the Heart: Short Stories from Latin America.* New York: Avon, 1973.

Translation

Tolstoy, Leo. *Anna Karenina.* Trans. David Magarshack. New York: Penguin, 1960.

No Author

Beowulf. Trans. David Wright. London: Penguin, 1960.

Corporate Author

Aurora Art and Hugh Lauter Levin Associates. *Impressionism and Post-Impression.* New York: Park Lane, 1989.

Multivolume Work

Durant, Will and Ariel. *The Story of Civilization.* 11 Vols. New York: Simon, 1965.

Book in a Series

Radloff, Bernhard. *Cosmopolis and Truth: Melville's Critique of Modernity.* Studies on Themes and Motifs in Literature 16. New York: Peter Lang, 1996.

Poem in an Anthology

Pound, Ezra. "The Seafarer." *A 20th Century Anthology.* Ed. W.E. Messenger and W.H. New. Scarborough, ON: Prentice, 1984. 68–70.

Edition

Shakespeare, William. *King Lear.* Ed. Alfred Harbage. London: Penguin, 1986.

Later Edition

Strunk, William Jr., and E.B. White. *The Elements of Style.* 4th ed. Boston: Allyn and Bacon, 2000.

Republished Book

Frost, Robert. *Poems.* 1916. New York: Washington Square, 1971.

Other Language

Kosok, Heinz. *Geschichte der anglo-irischen Literatur.* Berlin: Erich Schmidt, 1990.

Pamphlet

Johnston, Denis. *John Millington Synge.* Columbia Essays on Modern Writers 12. New York: Columbia UP, 1965.

Foreword/Introduction:

Franklin, Phyllis. Foreword. *MLA Handbook for Writers of Research Papers.* Ed. Joseph Gibaldi. New York: MLA, 1999. xiii-xviii.

REFERENCE BOOK

Young, Philip. "Hemingway, Ernest." *Encyclopedia Americana.* 2nd ed. 1973.

NEWSPAPER

Article

Jeffrey, David L. "Michael O'Brien: A Prophet in his own country." *Ottawa Citizen* 12 Apr. 1998: E1.

Editorial

"A toast to progress!" Editorial. *Globe and Mail* [Toronto] 30 Dec. 1999: A1.

Letter to the Editor

Tobin, Douglas W. Letter. *New York Times* 2 Jan. 2000, early ed., sec. 4: 8.

MAGAZINE

Matus, Irvin. "The Case for Shakespeare." *Atlantic* Oct. 1991: 64–72.

JOURNAL

Continuous Pagination

Marrouchi, M. Ben. "Literature is Dead, Long Live Theory." *Queen's Quarterly* 98 (1991): 775- 803.

Separate Pagination/New Series

Breslin, Paul. "Two Cheers For The New Formalism." *Kenyon Review* ns 13.2 (1991): 143-148. ("ns" indicates that it is a new series.)

Issue Numbers only

Hillger, Annick. "Afterbirth of Earth: Messianic Materialism in Anne Michaels' *Fugitive Pieces.*" *Canadian Literature* 160 (1999): 28-45.

DISSERTATION

Unpublished

Thornton, Patricia. "The Prison of Gender: Sexual Roles in Major American Novels of the 1920s." Diss. U of New Brunswick, 1976.

Published

Daigle, Marsha Ann. *Dante's "Divine Comedy" and the Fiction of C.S. Lewis.* Diss. U of Michigan, 1984. Ann Arbor: UMI, 1989.

Abstract

Linkskold, Jane M. "The Persephone Myth in D.H. Lawrence." Diss. Fordham U, 1989. *DAI* 49 (1989): 3733A.

REVIEW

Book

Towers, R. Rev. of *Friend of My Youth,* by Alice Munro. *New York Review of Books* 17 May 1990: 38-39.

Film

Ansen, David. "How the West was Lost." Rev. of *Dances with Wolves,* dir. Kevin Costner. *Newsweek* 19 Nov. 1990: 67-68.

Play

Portman, Jamie. "Shaw Festival does *Uncle Vanya* proud." Rev. of *Uncle Vanya,* by Anton Chekhov. Shaw Festival, Niagara-on-the-Lake. *Ottawa Citizen* 21 Aug. 1999: E12.

INTERVIEW

Personal

McCormick, Edwin. Personal interview. 10 Jan. 1980.

Published

Gordimer, Nadine. Interview. "The Power of a Well-Told Tale." By P. Gray and B. Nelan. *Time* 14 Oct. 1991: 91-92.

Radio/Television

Gordimer, Nadine. Interview. *Writers and Company.* By Eleanor Wachtel. CBC Stereo, Toronto. 26 May 1991.

Recorded

Munro, Alice. Interview. By Kay Bonetti. Audiocassette. American Audio Prose Library, 1987.

SPEECH/LECTURE

Peck, M. Scott. "A New Psychology of Love, Traditional Values and Spiritual Growth." Lecture Series. The Centre of New Fire. Congress Centre, Ottawa. 22 Sept. 1990.

CONFERENCE PROCEEDINGS

Staines, David, ed. *The Callaghan Symposium.* Proc. of a Conf., 24-25 Apr. 1980, U of Ottawa. Ottawa: Ottawa UP, 1981.

FILM/VIDEO

A Doll's House. Dir. Patrick Garland. Perf. Claire Bloom and Anthony Hopkins. South Gate Entertainment, 1989.

RADIO/TELEVISION PROGRAM

Disgrace. By J.M. Coetzee. *Talking Books.* Host Ian Brown. CBC Radio 1, Toronto. 7 Nov. 1999.

SOUND RECORDING

Shakespeare, William. *Coriolanus.* Perf. Richard Burton and Jessica Tandy. Dir. Howard Sackler. Audiocassette. Caedmon Audio, 1962.

PERFORMANCE

The Cherry Orchard. By Anton Chekhov. Trans. John Murrell. Dir. Diana Leblanc. Perf. Martha Henry. Tom Patterson Theatre, Stratford, ON. 4 July 1998.

WORK OF ART

Picasso, Pablo. *Still Life with Chair-Caning.* Musee Picasso, Paris.

PUBLISHED LETTER

Frost, Robert. "Letter to Editor of the *Independent.*" 28 Mar. 1894. *Selected Letters of Robert Frost.* Ed. Lawrence Thompson. New York: Holt, 1964. 19.

MANUSCRIPT

Hare, W.A. Diary. 1900. Hare Papers. National Archives, Ottawa.

CD-ROM

Vincent, Thomas, comp. *Index to Pre-1900 English Canadian Cultural and Literary Magazines.* CD-ROM. Ottawa: Optim, 1994.

MULTIPLE BOOKS BY THE SAME AUTHOR

When listing two or more books by the same author or editor, enter the name for the first entry only. For the next and successive entries, type three hyphens followed by a period. Then enter the title and publication details as explained in the preceding pages. Sources are entered in alphabetical order by title.

Gibaldi, Joseph, ed. *MLA Handbook for Writers of Research Papers.* 5th ed. New York: MLA, 1999.

- - - . *MLA Style Manual and Guide to Scholarly Publishing.* 2nd ed. New York: MLA, 1998.

All titles have been italicized in the above examples. If you are using a word processor, titles should be italicized. In handwritten or typed essays, titles italicized in this manual should be underlined.

Online Sources

Like print or video sources used in an essay, online material must also be documented. As explained on pages 127–131, there are major differences between traditional sources and online sources. Some of these differences directly influence documentation procedures.

Online sources are ephemeral — they may exist today and disappear tomorrow. Online sources are frequently updated and they can be easily modified by adding or deleting details. Furthermore, the access route and the address or URL may change. Because of their fleeting nature and ease of alteration, it is necessary to provide two dates when citing online sources — the date of publication followed by the date that you consulted the source. Since sources do frequently disappear or change drastically, you may wish to **print copies** of your online sources or, alternatively, **save them** to disk as confirmation of their existence. Consider printing just the first page of lengthy documents.

In printed sources, such as a book, a page reference in a citation indicates the specific location of important material used in the essay. But page numbers are seldom used in online documents. If possible, always try to identify the exact location of a source when citing in text by using a section heading, a chapter, or a paragraph number if a page reference is not available. This is not an issue restricted to online sources; some traditional sources, such as speeches, interviews, and films do not use page numbers either.

Accuracy of URL details is essential for online documentation because a missing letter or punctuation mark may prevent a reader from accessing a web site. When entering URLs, always enclose them in angle brackets. URLs can be lengthy and it is often necessary to continue on a second line. In such a case, break the URL after a punctuation mark, such as a slash. At all costs, avoid hyphenating any split words.

Otherwise you should follow the same principles for documenting your sources as explained earlier in this section. For example, you follow similar procedures for citing in text as shown on pages 96–98. On the following pages we have illustrated the procedures for listing a variety of online sources using MLA principles.

Scholarly Database

Project Bartleby. Ed. Steven van Leeuwen. Oct. 1999. Columbia U. 3 Jan. 2000 <http://www.columbia.edu/acis/bartleby/>.

Professional Site

Russell, Yvan. *The Anton Chekhov Page.* 19 April 1998. 3 Jan. 2000 <http://eldred.ne.mediaone.net/ac/yr/Anton Chekhov.html>.

Question and Answer Database

Seiler, Edward and John H. Jenkins. *Frequently Asked Questions about Isaac Asimov.* 2 April 1999. 3 Jan. 2000 <http://www.clark. net/pub/edseiler/WWW/asimov_FAQ.html>.

Reference Work

"Chekhov, Anton." *Britannica.com.* 1999. By Ronald Hingley. Encyclopaedia Britannica. 2 Jan. 2000 <http://www.britannica.com/ bcom/eb/article/0/0,5716,23120+3,00.html>.

Newspaper Article

Zane, J. Peder. "Zane's View: The End of the Literature Era?" *Naples Daily News* 29 Jan. 1999. 2 Jan. 2000 <http://www.naplesnews. com/special/books/99/jan/a00z29.htm>.

Newsletter

Hamilton, Eric. "Making Choices, Creating Opportunities." *History Now* Spring (1997). 12 Jan. 1999   <http://hss.cmu.edu/HTML/ departsments/history/Spring97_1.html>.

Magazine

Murphy, Cait. "Ulysses in Chinese." *Atlantic Monthly* Sept. 1995. 2 Jan. 2000 <http://www.theatlantic.com/issues/95sep/ulyss.htm>.

Journal

Menichetti, David. "German Policy in Occupied Belgium." *Essays in History* 39 (1997). 11 Jan. 1999   <http://etext.lib.virginia.edu/journals/EH/EH39/menich39.html>.

Slides/Photographs

Leo Tolstoy with Anton Chekhov. N.d.   3   Jan.   2000 <http://www.pitzer.edu/~dward/Anarchist_Archives/bright/tolstoy/ graphics/lt_chekov.jpg>.

Sound

Joyce, James. "Joyce reads from the *Wake.*" *Work in Progress.* N.d. 3 Jan. 2000 <http://www.2street.com/joyce/gallery/joycevoice. html>.

Film Review

Ebert, Roger. Rev. of *Shakespeare in Love*, dir. John Madden. *Roger Ebert on Movies* Dec. 1998. 2 Jan. 2000 <http://www.suntimes. com/ebert/ebert_reviews/1998/12/122505.html>.

Book Review

Rahv, Philip. "House of the Dead?" Rev. of *One Day in the Life of Ivan Denisovich*, by Alexander Solzhenitsyn. *New York Review of Books* Feb.1963. 3 Jan. 2000 <http://www.nybooks.com/nyrev/WWWfirstdisplay.cgi?19630200004R1>.

TV/Radio Program

Allison, Jay. "Mr. Watson, Come Here, I Want You!" *Lost & Found Sound.* Natl. Public Radio. 19 March 1999. 6 May 1999 <http://www.npr.org/programs/lnfsound/onair/990319.onair. html>.

Art

da Vinci, Leonardo. *The Mona Lisa.* 1506. Louvre, Paris. 2 Jan. 2000 <http://mistral.culture.fr/louvre/anglais/collec/peint/inv0779/peint_f.htm>.

Interview

Atwood, Margaret. Interview with Laura Miller. *Salon Magazine.* January 1997. 2 Jan. 2000 <http://www.salonmagazine.com/jan97/interview970120.html>.

Book

Dickens, Charles. *Great Expectations.* 1861. 2 Jan. 2000 <http://www.bibliomania.com/Fiction/dickens/greatexp/index.html>.

Book (Translation)

Tolstoy, Leo. *Resurrection.* Trans. Louise Maude. N.d. 1 June 1999 <ftp://beta.ulib.org/webRoot/Books/_Gutenberg_Etext_Books_NEWEST/etext99/resur10.txt>.

Poem

Walker, Margaret. *For My People.* 1942. 1 Dec. 1999 <http://metalab.unc.edu/ipa/walker/formypeople.html>.

Play

Shakespeare, William. *Much Ado About Nothing.* 1598. 15 Dec. 1999 <http://www-tech.mit.edu/Shakespeare/Comedy/muchadoaboutnothing/muchadoaboutnothing.html>.

Electronic Mail

Snelgrove, M. "Background info on main characters." E-mail to J.S. Henderson. 5 Jan. 2000.

Software Program

APA Style Helper. Vers. I.0. 1998. 5 Jan. 1999 <http://www.apa.org/apa-style/>.

Personal Web Site

Hunt, Andrew. *Andrew's Diner.* N.d. 18 Jan. 1999 <http://www.arts.uwaterloo.ca/~aehunt/>.

The list of sources for the Chekhov essay is laid out in MLA style below. You will notice that it is designated "Works Consulted" not "Works Cited." This is because the list of sources includes both cited works as well as additional sources that proved useful in preparing the essay.

Works Consulted

Chekhov, Anton. *Five Plays*. Trans. Ronald Hingley. Oxford: Oxford UP, 1977.

Gilman, Richard. *Chekhov's Plays: An Opening into Eternity*. New Haven, CT: Yale UP, 1995.

Kelly, Eileen. "Chekhov the Subversive." *New York Review of Books* 6 Nov. 1997: 61-66.

Meister, Charles. *Chekhov Criticism, 1880 through 1986*. Jefferson, NC: McFarland, 1988.

Peace, Richard. *Chekhov, a Study of the Four Major Plays*. New Haven, CT: Yale UP, 1983.

Troyat, Henri. *Chekhov*. Trans. Michael H. Heim. London: MacMillan, 1987.

Uncle Vanya. By Anton Chekhov. Trans. John Murrell. Dir. Ian Prinsloo. Court House Theatre, Niagara-on-the-Lake. 25 Sept. 1999.

Vanya on 42nd Street. Dir. Louis Malle. Malofilm, 1995.

Vitins, I. "Uncle Vanya's Predicament." *Slavic and East European Journal* 22 (1978): 454-63.

Notes

MLA recommends that two types of supplementary notes be used with parenthetical citations: content notes and bibliographic notes.

- **Content notes** contain explanatory information. While this information might be relevant to the essay, it could detract from the development of your argument if inserted directly in the text. For example, a content note might explain that there is some question as to the precise publication date of the literary work that is the subject of your essay.

- **Bibliographic notes** are used for critical comments on sources or for suggesting additional sources to consult for further details.

When using these notes, place a superscript number at the appropriate place in the text. Then write the note after the corresponding number, either at the bottom of the page as a footnote, as shown in the examples below, or on a separate page at the end of the essay as an endnote. Notes are numbered consecutively throughout the paper. It is more convenient for the reader to refer to explanatory and bibliographic information at the bottom of the page than to turn

Example:

[1] To show the Duke's aggrandizing nature in his production of the play, the director, Jonathan Miller, made Isabella march off the stage when the Duke announced their marriage (McLuskie 95).

[2] For other examples of verbal echoes of *Hamlet* and *Lord Jim*, see Part 2 of *Conrad and Shakespeare and Other Essays* by Adam Gillon.

to the end of the essay. This is especially true when reading dissertations in microform. Word processing programs make it relatively easy to use the footnote format.

Footnotes are separated from the text by a solid line twenty spaces in length. Leave a blank line and then indent five spaces or a single tab space. Type the number in superscript followed by a space and then the note. If the note continues beyond one line, start subsequent lines at the left margin. Single-space any notes that continue on a second line, but leave a double space between individual notes. It is also acceptable to use a slightly smaller font size for your footnotes than the regular type used in the essay. The footnote format is demonstrated on the previous page, showing an example of a content note first, followed by a bibliographic note.

Another method is to place all content and bibliographic notes on a separate page at the end of the essay just before the list of sources. Title the page "Notes" and enter the details as explained above for footnotes. For endnotes you may double-space throughout and use the same font size as in the essay.

You must resist the temptation to place too much information in content or bibliographic notes because constant reference to footnotes or endnotes may distract the reader from the development of your argument in the text of the essay. Ask yourself whether the information is essential to the argument. If not, eliminate it. If it is, consider incorporating the information in the text before creating a note. In the case of lengthy information, consider placing it in the appendix instead of creating a note. Whichever method you use for content and bibliographic notes, it is important that you strive for **consistency, simplicity, and clarity**. If in doubt about the need for explanatory and bibliographic information, always consult your instructor.

If you are using the numbered footnote/endnote procedure for documenting your sources (as used throughout *The English Essay*), you will notice that explanatory information is indicated, not by a number, but by an asterisk or similar symbol as shown on page 39. The difference between explanatory notes and citation (or documentary) notes is explained in *The Research Essay*.

STYLE

Style is the manner of your writing rather than the substance of your essay. It is the written expression of your ideas, not the ideas themselves, or as Lucile Payne puts it: "It is the 'how' (form) as opposed to the 'what' (content)."[12] Every person's writing style is unique. Although your style reflects your personality, your style must still be governed by the conventions of language usage. You cannot adopt a style that departs drastically from orthodox sentence structure and commonly accepted forms of punctuation if you wish to communicate successfully. Many manuals have been published on English usage and writing style. This book does not claim to be a style manual. However, this section does offer some practical tips on how to become proficient at the craft of writing essays and thereby shape a clear and smooth personal style.

Reading

Read as many books and magazines as you can. Read widely, from the classics to contemporary literature. If you find a particular piece of writing effective, try to determine why it is effective. If you encounter new words, as you undoubtedly will, add them to your vocabulary. Reading the editorials in reputable newspapers and magazines is good training for essay writing, since editorials are often mini-essays with arguments based on evidence. Remember that reading, writing, and thinking are inseparably linked.

Writing

Experiment with the different writing techniques that you have identified through your reading.

Writing is not an innate gift — it is a craft that must be learned. It is worth noting that there is no literary equivalent to the genius of a Mozart, who amazed the crowned heads of Europe with his talent at the age of five. It is usually only after many years of hard work that great writers make their mark. Like sports stars and chess players, good writers develop their craft through practice and persistence. As with most skills, successful style is usually only ten percent inspiration and ninety percent perspiration.

Clarity

Clarity of expression is one of the key features of a successful style. Brevity, simplicity, and precision are the essential qualities of clear style. Prune ruthlessly as you edit your draft and eliminate the clutter of foggy phrases such as "at that point in time" or "by the same token."[13] "Etcetera/ (etc.)" is a meaningless term and should never be used. Likewise, words such as "hopefully" and "meaningful" do little to clarify meaning. Always be aware of your readers — they want clarity, not confusion.

Vocabulary

The development and expression of an idea depend largely on your selection and use of words. Judicious selection of words not only ensures clarity of meaning, it also enhances the sound and harmony of your writing. Words are the bricks of language. Enhance your vocabulary by jotting down in a journal any new words and their meanings that you encounter in your reading. Build lists of similar-looking words that cause confusion, such as "flaunt" and "flout," "enormity" and "enormous," and "imply" and "infer." You can also create lists of synonyms and antonyms to expand your vocabulary. Always choose concrete words over vague terms and abstract generalizations in your writing. A reputable dictionary and a thesaurus or dictionary of synonyms are essential companions for a writer.

Fluency

Good writing has an even flow. Give your writing rhythm and harmony by your choice of words and your use of punctuation. For instance, you can use transitional words such as "nevertheless," "consequently," and "furthermore" to link the flow of ideas; and you can use punctuation structures — such as a series of clauses linked by semi-colons — to present your ideas to their best advantage. Test your writing for eloquence by reading it aloud and then fine-tune it until it flows smoothly and naturally.

Tone

An essay is a work of ideas, not moods or feelings. A style of expression that is appropriate for writing a short story is not appropriate for writing an academic essay. An essay is a serious piece of writing; therefore, the tone should be formal and scholarly, but not dull and boring. As your writing skills improve, you will find that your writing can be formal and scholarly and still be colourful and witty.

Contractions such as "can't" and "won't" should not be used in formal writing, even though they are part of everyday speech. Likewise, slang, jargon, and trendy, overused expressions, such as "prioritize," have no place in an essay.

Jargon

Every academic discipline has its own jargon and code words. Some of these words are necessary and useful, since they can define a concept with great precision, but some of them are no more than big words designed to impress a reader. These words usually obscure the meaning of the essay. A good essay is not something written in a secret code that only the writer and the instructor can understand; a good essay should be accessible to any intelligent reader.

Discriminatory Language

Never use language that discriminates on the grounds of sex, race, or religion. Language that stereotypes people and groups is unacceptable in any type of writing. In particular, avoid using the masculine pronoun when referring to human groups that could legitimately be male or female, or comprised of both sexes. Guides are available to help you substitute words and expressions that are free of discrimination.

Pronouns

Instructors do not agree on the use of pronouns in essays. Some accept the use of the first person "I," others reject its use. Some prefer "the author" or "the writer," while others regard these terms as pretentious. "We" or "one" find acceptance with some instructors, but not with others. However, there is near unanimity on avoiding the use of the second person pronoun "you" in formal academic writing. ("You" is used frequently in this book because it is an instructional manual.) Always clarify the preferences of your instructors about the use of pronouns.

Grammar

Language is based on rules and conventions that serve to clarify comprehension. If you ignore rules and conventions, you will only obscure the meaning of your essay. Develop a sound knowledge of basic grammar and do not simply rely on a computer grammar check program.

Sentences

Vary the length of your sentences to change the pace of your writing. Shorter sentences can be used to give emphasis to a point. Further emphasis can be given by placing the key words at the end of the sentence. Make sure that every sentence really is a sentence, with a proper subject and a verb.

Punctuation

Pay attention to punctuation. Good punctuation can improve the readability and clarity of your essay to a remarkable degree. Since an essay is a formal piece of writing, do not use the exclamation mark and minimize the use of the dash.

Verbs

Literary essays are written in the present tense, unlike other essays. Literary texts are not historical texts, nor are literary characters dead — they spring to life in the imagination of every reader who picks up a text. Consequently, Hamlet "is" ambivalent, not "was" ambivalent.

Only use the past tense when you are making some type of historical reference, such as "*The Apprenticeship of Duddy Kravitz* was Mordecai Richler's first commercially successful novel."

Give added force to your writing by using active, not passive, verbs where possible, such as "Charles Dickens wrote *Hard Times* as a criticism of the evils of industrialization," rather than "*Hard Times* was written by Charles Dickens as a criticism of the evils of industrialization." Guard against an increasing tendency to use nouns as verbs. For example, "impact" and "dialogue" are nouns, not verbs — "to impact" and "to dialogue" do not exist.

Spelling

Careless spelling can mar an otherwise well-written essay. Use a dictionary and the spell check function on the computer to correct errors. No spelling errors should slip through the final proofreading.

A pleasing style is not based solely on rigid and mechanically correct English. Attempt to breathe vigour and vitality into your writing. Do not be discouraged if your first efforts do not create the effects that you want: developing a good writing style requires dedication and application, effort and practice. But the payoff is worth it, for a pleasing style will not only enhance the clarity of your essay, it will also add a persuasive element to your arguments. **More importantly, a lucid writing style is a lifelong asset.**

CONCLUSION

An essay is an exploration into unknown territory. As on all journeys of discovery, you will experience both elation and tribulation, fascination and frustration. The excitement of analyzing texts and gaining new insights will frequently be offset by the difficulties of meeting deadlines, structuring arguments, and crafting ideas into words. There is no "quick fix" formula for preparing quality assignments; however, with practice, patience, and persistence you will overcome the obstacles that you encounter.

This manual has outlined a process that follows a systematic and logical progression from the first step of selecting a topic through to the final submission of the completed assignment. The different stages in the process give direction to your assignment and allow you to plan your work. Advance planning is critical, since you are unlikely to learn much, derive any satisfaction, or achieve any success if your essay is written in frenzied haste the night before the assignment is due. Samuel Johnson's comment that "what is written without effort is in general read without pleasure" is as valid today as it was two hundred years ago.

The process, however, is not always as linear and sequential as represented in a diagram. Frequently, you will deviate from the pathway and loop back as you develop and refine your response to a text. The process is flexible, so modify it and shape your own pathways for preparing your assignments. The pathways might vary slightly, but whether you are writing an 800-word essay on a single literary text, a poetry commentary in an examination, or a 2000-word research paper, the destination is the same: a clear, coherent, and convincing presentation of your point of view.

While it is important to have a method to process information and ideas, fundamental to any process is the depth and precision of your thinking: think creatively to brainstorm new insights and generate imaginative questions; think critically to evaluate ideas and assess arguments; and think logically to construct a clear and convincing thesis. Discuss, question, read, and write to develop and sharpen all aspects of your thinking. The English novelist E.M. Forster reminds us of the link between writing and thinking: "how do we know what we think until we see what we have written?" Therefore, it is important to develop a proficient command of language to express with clarity and precision the thoughts and ideas generated by your analysis and research.

Finally, remember that it is your response and your insights that are important — not a dry recitation of what others have written about a literary work. Although a text like *Hamlet* has been interpreted by scholars and students for centuries, you can still provide original insights. Interpretations are never final; they are tentative probings at understanding works of literature. It is on the accumulated insights and interpretations of myriads of writers that knowledge is built; you are part of the building process.

Appendix

1. Research Aids

Computers facilitate the research process by providing access to local databases, the Internet, and CD-ROM databases.

- Most libraries have replaced their card catalogues with databases of computer-readable records accessible through terminals onsite. These **local** or internal databases contain details of each library's holdings.

- The explosion of the **Internet** enables researchers to search resources around the world with ease and speed. These online or external resources comprise both full-text material, such as newspapers, as well as bibliographic citation databases, such as periodical indexes.

- Many databases have been converted to **CD-ROM** format. Like Internet resources, CD-ROM versions provide both full-text sources and searching capabilities. CD-ROM databases are available through networked systems or stand-alone stations in many libraries.

Information technology, while offering exciting opportunities for researchers, also contains potential pitfalls. The Internet is not a library; it is more like a gigantic electronic bookstore where not only are the titles listed, but the contents of many documents are also available. Library resources and catalogues are compiled by specialists, whereas searches on the Internet usually return sources compiled by a computer program. As a result, the classification of online material is often inconsistent and haphazard. Therefore, you may score thousands of "hits," many irrelevant, when doing a keyword search.

There are other limitations, such as copyright, which restrict the number of quality "publications" available on the Internet. Another limitation is access to some of the best bibliographic and full-text databases because the information providers charge fees. The Internet does offer free material, but some of it is of dubious quality.

Despite these limitations, computers provide some distinct advantages for developing a comprehensive Working Bibliography. Besides speedy access to material, you can search by keyword or use Boolean logic to narrow your search. Many search engines also have help pages with advice on research methods. Libraries often have web sites listing resources that have been compiled by specialists. Some sites, devoted to academic topics and authors, are maintained by professors and librarians.

Since cyberspace is an environment in constant flux, it is impossible to provide current and comprehensive details on using the Internet. Consult guides such as *Online!*, or speak to librarians, and check web sites that offer practical advice. Remember, however, that the Internet is only one tool in your kit of research skills.

Computer techniques can complement traditional searching methods. In some instances the two overlap. For example, many printed works, such as books and encyclopedias, are available on both CD-ROM and online. In other areas the two formats have each developed their own niche. For example, many printed works will never be digitized because of copyright restrictions, while many online documents are never printed because they become dated quickly or because of cost. While most indexes are produced in electronic form today, the early volumes are usually only available in print. When building your Working Bibliography, use strategies that include both traditional methods and the latest technology.

On the following pages you will find a comprehensive list of research aids. These resources are supplemented with examples that may be in formats as varied as print, microform, audio-visual, online, or CD-ROM. For additional information on searching methods and for a discussion of the merits of the "real" and the "virtual" library, there is no better resource to consult than Thomas Mann's excellent guide which is listed in the Works Consulted on page 153.

- The catalogue is the main source of information about the library's resources. Computer catalogues offer greater versatility for searching than the traditional author/title and subject divisions of the card system. For example, you can search by a keyword in the title. Enter the name "Chekhov" and the computer will list all works with "Chekhov" in the title, regardless of the position of the word.

- Since the richness of language usually permits a concept to be expressed in a number of ways, it is possible that subject terms familiar to you may not be the ones selected by the author for the title. In order to help you find works on the same subject, the Library of Congress devised the *Library of Congress Subject Headings (LCSH)*. If you look up the term "literary movements" in the *LCSH*, for example, you will find a number of related headings that you can use in your searching.

- Although it may seem old-fashioned in the age of computer technology, browsing in the library stacks can be an effective means of expanding your list of sources. You can locate your "browsing area" by using the *LCSH* and the catalogue to determine which stacks hold books on your topic. By running your eye along the shelves you will often discover useful sources. And by checking tables of contents and indexes you will often pinpoint pertinent information in sources that would not be revealed in a catalogue search. A careful scrutiny of bibliographies and references in books on related topics will often turn up additional sources.

- The reference shelves, containing a wide assortment of material, can be a profitable area for browsing.

  Handbooks, e.g. *A Handbook to English Literature*

  Dictionaries, e.g. *Dictionary of Literary Biography*

  Encyclopedias, e.g. *Cambridge Encyclopedia of Language*

  Concordances, e.g. *A Concordance to the Poems of Robert Browning*

  Guides are available to assist you in determining the availability of reference material on your topic:

  Guide to Reference Books

  Walford's Guide to Reference Material

- Periodical indexes and abstracts are essential tools because they enable you to locate articles in hundreds of popular magazines and scholarly journals. The basic difference between abstracts and indexes is that the former not only provide citations for the articles but also summarize the subject matter. The following are just a few that are useful for research into literature:

Humanities Index

Abstracts of English Studies

Short Story Index

Periodical indexes can be either specific, such as the *Play Index* or general, such as the *Humanities Index*. It is even possible to delve into journals and magazines in the nineteenth century by using *Poole's Index to Periodical Literature* or *Wellesley's Index to Victorian Periodicals*. The *Essay and General Literature Index* is similar to a periodical index, except that it identifies essays and articles in published anthologies.

- Citation indexes stand in a class of their own. Even though they can be used for a subject search, they really enable the researcher to identify who has been cited by a given author by providing lists of cited references. *The Arts and Humanities Citation Index* is a useful tool for advanced literature research.

- Bibliographies are publications listing books, articles, and other sources on specific topics. They are especially useful because someone else has done the searching for you.

Bibliography: Women and Language

A Shakespeare Bibliography

The Bibliographic Index is a subject list of bibliographies published separately or as part of books and articles.

- Book reviews may enable you to determine the reliability of a book, and they will often provide additional information and insights on your subject.

Book Review Digest

Index to Book Reviews in the Humanities

Many periodical and newspaper indexes have sections on book reviews.

- Newspapers are a valuable source of information. The following is a sample of many newspaper indexes that will give you quick access to articles and editorials:

  Index to the Times

  New York Times Index

- A number of publications provide annual reviews of developments in their disciplines or commentaries on publications published during the year.

  These include:

  American Literary Scholarship

  Annual Bulletin of Historical Literature

- Biographical indexes are indispensable if you are studying an individual. These include:

  Contemporary Authors

  Biography Index

- Masters theses and doctoral dissertations are useful for both content details as well as source information in their bibliographies.

  Canadian Theses

  Dissertation Abstracts Ondisc

- Some publications, such as the following, outline research aids and important works in the study of literature and language.

  A Guide to English and American Literature

  Literary Research Guide

- Many speeches, lectures, and papers are delivered each year at conferences and conventions. Transcripts are often made available and they are accessible through indexes such as the following:

  Bibliographic Guide to Conference Publications

  Directory of Published Proceedings

- If you do not read other languages, you can still gain access to other cultures and perspectives by using the following guides to works in translation:

  Translations Register-Index

  Journals in Translation

- Much information is stored on microfiche and microfilm for preservation purposes and in order to save space. Material in microform includes out-of-print books, newspapers, periodicals, dissertations, and pamphlets. Microforms in the library are usually accessible through the catalogue. There are also guides to microform material, such as the following:

  Microform Research Collections: A Guide

  Subject Guide to Microforms in Print

- There is a wide range of non-print material available in the form of photographs, taped interviews, films, television, and radio programs. The following are just a few of numerous databases, indexes, and catalogues:

  A-V Online

  Shakespeare on Screen

  Bowker's Complete Video Directory

  The Media Review Digest

  Many libraries have special audio-visual rooms with catalogues and equipment. Holdings may include films, slides, filmstrips, records, compact discs, laser discs, and video and audio cassettes. Some libraries even permit loans.

- The current interest in oral history has resulted in many libraries and archives developing collections of audio-taped material. Refer to guides such as *Oral History Collections and Oral History: A Reference Guide and Annotated Bibliography* to determine the accessibility of oral material pertinent to your project. *Words On Cassette* is an extensive bibliography of material on audio-cassette.

- Professors, teachers, and librarians with special interests can provide useful leads. You can also contact experts by e-mail or raise questions through discussion groups or listservs on the Internet.

- Your library will not contain all existing publications, but an inter-library loan system facilitates obtaining material from other libraries. Electronic networks allow libraries to determine the location of a specific source quickly. Copies of journal articles can be obtained through a document delivery service. Approach your librarian if you wish to use these services.

2.   Sources

The sources that you use to prepare your essay and from which you draw the information and ideas needed to develop your arguments will comprise one or more of three different types: primary, secondary, and tertiary.

Primary sources are original records and material, and include the accounts of eyewitnesses, personal memoirs and literary works. Primary material may be in published form, such as an autobiography or a play, but much primary information is often unpublished, such as letters, diaries, and taped interviews. Primary material may also be in non-print form such as customs, traditions, legends, and folklore. Primary sources also include original films, live performances, photographs, and works of art.

A major problem facing writers when handling primary material is the authenticity of their sources and the reliability of the information. Is a manuscript perhaps a forgery? Does a diarist have concealed motives? How trustworthy is the autobiography of a prominent writer? Has a photograph been reconstructed? Has a painting been forged? How selective is the editing of a documentary film? What is fact and what is fiction?

Verifying (determining authenticity) and evaluating (determining reliability) are important facets of research and writing. Most students will not have the time nor the expertise to verify unpublished primary sources, such as determining the authenticity of a Shakespeare manuscript. The problem of authenticity does not arise — or only rarely arises — with published primary texts. However, the reliability of the version of the text that you are using is an important issue.

The original language of a literary work is often modernized by editors in later versions. While you should always try to get as close as possible to the original language, you should also be aware of later critical editions with modifications and comments on the original version. Consult your instructors and book reviews to determine the reliability of different versions of a literary work.

Translations pose similar problems, so once again you should consult instructors and book reviews about reputable and authoritative editions.

Initially you will be working with a single primary text: the literary work that is the focus of your essay. As you progress with your assignments, your instructor might ask you to supplement your analysis of a primary text with other primary sources. For example, if you were to focus on a play by a major contemporary playwright you could consult or view (if available and accessible) some of the following primary sources in addition to the text:

- a live performance of the play
- a film or video of the play
- a documentary film about the playwright
- a reading by the playwright
- a taped interview with the playwright
- a speech (live, taped, or printed) by the playwright
- published correspondence of the playwright
- an autobiography
- an online discussion hosted by the playwright
- a thesis or dissertation by the playwright
- newspaper or journal articles by the playwright
- published photographs

Secondary sources are based on primary material. They are written at a later date than the primary sources on which they are based and from which they draw their conclusions. Secondary sources present another person's interpretation of the primary material, and they often develop an argument or point of view. A work of literary criticism is an example of a secondary source.

Using secondary critical studies is a double-edged sword. On the one hand, you can benefit from the insights and interpretations of critics as you shape and refine your own responses to the text. Evaluating the interpretations and judgments of scholars also enables you to sharpen your critical talents. On the other hand, blind reliance on and regurgitation of secondary comments can blunt the development of initiative and independence, insight, and imagination.

Most of your secondary sources will probably be in the form of books and articles and, increasingly, electronic documents. Commercial "Notes" on literary works are widely available and they represent a certain type of secondary source. Authenticity of secondary sources is seldom a problem, but the credibility and reliability of the material or the views expressed may be questionable.

Questions such as the following will help you determine the reliability of your secondary sources:

- How well known is the author?

- How reputable is the publishing company?

- Is the article published in a respected journal?

- How recently was it published?

- How frequently is the author cited in other sources?

- Can important information be confirmed by another source?

- Does the author treat the subject fairly?

- Are the interpretations and arguments well-supported and appropriately documented?

- Is the tone and style both formal and correct?

- Has a critical work been positively reviewed in a journal or newspaper?

Tertiary sources are works that summarize primary and secondary material and provide broad overviews of the information; examples are encyclopedias and other reference works. Tertiary sources are especially useful for the preliminary and preparatory reading, but they have limited value as material for the detailed research.

Electronic, or digital, sources can be divided into two main groups: online material available through the Internet and portable databases, such as CD-ROMs, which may be shared via a network. CD-ROMs are not as current as online databases, but they can be consulted at no cost in many libraries. Both CD-ROMs and online sources may include primary, secondary, and tertiary material and they are available in formats as varied as text, video, sound, and graphics. Many electronic sources are identical to print versions, while others are only available in digital form, such as online journals and magazines known as e-zines.

Sources in digital form offer many advantages, such as:

- Easy storage of large volumes of information.
- Quick access and retrieval of information.
- Enhancing print versions of documents by adding sound and images.

Online sources have certain distinct advantages, such as current information and hyperlinks that allow for instantaneous connections to related web documents. Another advantage is the variety of material and activities available on the Internet.

- You can access primary material in museums, galleries, and archives.
- You can search library catalogues and databases around the world.
- You can discuss problems with other students and even with experts.

A major difference between online sources and traditional sources is the ease and speed with which online material can be altered. This "invisible revisability"[14] creates a number of problems for researchers, such as documenting online sources as explained on pages 106–109.

The proliferation of online sources and their ease of access has produced a superabundance of information — much of questionable quality. While there are many excellent resources, there are also many dubious databases and web sites. Unlike a printed source, such as a book, which is expensive to publish, an online document can be "published" with relative ease and minimal expense. Furthermore, there is no quality control on the Internet. Online resources are not carefully selected by librarians, as are resources in a library. Therefore, it is especially important to determine the quality of your online sources and to establish their authenticity and reliability.

Many of the criteria for evaluating traditional primary and secondary sources can be applied to online sources. Use the criteria and questions listed earlier with the suggestions below to judge your online material. You will also find useful advice on assessing Internet sources by searching online under "evaluating sources." Remember that a discriminating and critical user of information is always a more credible and respected writer.

- Can you find information to confirm that the author is reputable?

- Can you find other documents written by the author?

- Is the document published by a recognized organization?

- How recently was the document published or revised?

- What audience is the document addressing?

- On what type of site is the document published?

- What is the purpose of the document?

- How accurate is the information and can it be verified?

- Are there signs of bias in the document?

- What is the point of view of the author?

- Are there links to other reputable sources?

- Is there a bibliography of reliable sources?

Examine your online material thoroughly and filter the information with caution. Be vigilant: question and think continuously as you read and research. Mindlessly downloading undigested data from the Internet and then pasting it into essay format does not constitute critical thinking, and, without acknowledgment, may well constitute plagiarism. **The computer is simply a tool and its effectiveness as a tool is determined by how you use it.**

Ensure that your Working Bibliography includes a wide range of sources encompassing both the latest online information and traditional sources that reflect primary, secondary, and tertiary material. **Evaluate all your sources carefully for authenticity and reliability.**

3. The Abstract

An abstract forces the writer to examine closely the organization, argument, and presentation of the essay. It can also enhance the overall impression that your paper creates. It is written in concise essay form of between 100 and 300 words, and placed on the page immediately following the title page. Short abstracts of about 100 words are sometimes placed on the title page. Ask your instructor whether an abstract is required and, if so, what the specific requirements are and where it should be placed. The abstract is a short synopsis of the essay and, therefore, it must be written last. It must not be confused with the introduction, with which there might, however, be some overlap. The abstract may include all or some of the following features:

- Discussion of the topic of the essay and the selection of a specific problem or issue and its importance as a field for investigation.

- A clear statement of the essay's purpose or the research question.

- A statement of the thesis or argument and an explanation of the structure for the development of the thesis/argument.

- The conclusions reached.

- A definition of the limits of the assignment; a clarification of what is and is not being considered.

- A discussion of the various sources, primary and secondary, and their usefulness, as well as the research aids and libraries used.

- The documentation system and the nature of the list of sources, such as an annotated bibliography, for example, and whether explanatory footnotes or endnotes have been used.

- A list of the contents of the appendix.

The question you should ask yourself is this: If the essay is lost and only the abstract survives, will it convey to the reader a clear picture of the essay, its central argument, and its organization?

4.   EXAMINATIONS

Introduction

Instructors frequently use the essay format when setting examinations, whether they are take-home examinations or examinations written under supervision. Essay-style examinations can measure a wide range of skills, including:

- Addressing and interpreting a question.
- Developing and substantiating an argument.
- The logical organization of ideas.
- Clear, precise expression.
- Critical judgment.
- Thinking clearly under time constraints.

These skills cannot be demonstrated in a knowledge vacuum: a sound grasp of the basic course material and the theoretical framework is essential. **Knowledge and skills are inseparable in the writing of good essay answers.** There are many similarities between the major and minor term essays and the examination essay, though the scale may be different. The best practice for writing successful essay examinations is to develop and refine your thinking and writing skills during the course of the academic year — and the best preparation for an examination starts on the first day of the course.

Discuss with your instructor well before the examination:

- What will be covered and what will not be covered in the examination.
- The precise meaning of common examination terms.
- What criteria will be used in assessing the answers.
- Whether the questions have to be answered in the order in which they appear on the examination paper.
- Whether you should double-space or single-space your writing.

- Any other matters, such as the use of the first person pronoun.

Read the entire examination paper slowly.

- Pay careful attention to all the instructions. For example, confusing compulsory and optional questions could be disastrous.

- Read the questions carefully, underlining keywords, such as "analyze" and "discuss."

- Think carefully before selecting your questions (if a choice is permitted).

Consider the following before you start writing:

- Map out a schedule for answering the questions by allocating your time according to the marks awarded for each question. Allow time at the end for proofreading.

- If you are permitted to answer questions in any order, do those that you know best first.

- Do not waste your time writing out the questions; just number your answers correctly.

Approach each question carefully.

- Determine the precise meaning of keywords, such as "discuss" and "analyze." Misinterpreting important terms could create problems.

- Address the question exactly as it is phrased. Do not sidestep the question or substitute a title of your own creation.

- Never change a question to suit a prepared answer.

- Think carefully before tackling each question. Attempt a fresh interpretation.

- **Plan your answers.** Brainstorm the question and jot down relevant ideas and information. Then arrange a Basic Outline using the ABC formula, followed by a brief Skeleton Outline with supporting details, before you start.

- **Never** write a rough draft and then a good copy. Use your time more profitably. You can ensure neatness, organization, and accuracy by thoughtful planning and careful proofreading.

Reflect on the structure of the answer.

- Keep the introduction short. Brief background information and a clear thesis statement (response to the question) is all that is needed for an examination introduction. Some instructors prefer just a statement of the thesis and no background information.

- Develop and substantiate your thesis/argument/answer/point of view in the body.

- Complete your answer with a brief concluding paragraph in which you draw together the main threads of your answer and drive home your argument.

- Use your Basic Outline for each answer as a formula for shaping the paragraph structure. Avoid subheadings.

- Write in a clear and formal style. Precise, articulate expression has persuasive power.

The body is the most important part of an examination answer.

- You have limited time, so you must select just the essential and relevant information needed to support your answer.

- Focus on your thesis and ensure that all the information is linked explicitly to it. Simply pouring out all you know on a topic will destroy the clarity of your answer.

- Convincing interpretations, judgments, and arguments have to be anchored in solid evidence and concrete examples.

- Give your answers depth and detail and avoid vague generalities.

- Ensure that there is a logical sequence to the development of your ideas.

- Avoid speculating and conjecturing about hypothetical situations. "What if . . ." has no place in an answer.

- Do not try to force memorized quotations into your answers. If, however, you have remembered lines relevant to your answer, then by all means use them.

Remember that examiners reward thoughtful, lucid essays.

- Developing a clear and convincing response to each question is your sole task. The clarity of your answer is shaped largely by its structure and style.

- Examiners are looking for incisive analysis and argument, not for summaries of texts and superficial surveys.

- Remember the cliché: quality, not quantity. It is true.

- **Write legibly.** A paper that is easy to read will have a positive impact on the examiner. Avoid using correcting fluid and asterisks and arrows to make changes and additions.

- Number your pages accurately.

Watch the clock.

- Follow the time schedule you mapped out at the beginning of the examination.

- Allow time at the end to proofread your answers. Remember that proofreading is fine-tuning, not major revising.

- Complete the paper. Do not leave a scribbled list of points at the end with an apology to the examiner that you ran out of time. Examiners never accept that excuse. **Completing an examination within the time limit is part of the test.**

Do not panic if you are confronted by a difficult paper. Scour the depths of your memory for all relevant information and plan an outline. You can probably squeeze through in a crisis with a moderate amount of knowledge, good organization, and polished writing skills. Any attempt is better than no attempt at all.

Essays

Supervised examinations containing essay-style questions can take different forms:

- open-book
- notes permitted
- no notes permitted
- the question assigned in advance by the teacher
- design your own question and prepare your response in advance
- no advance knowledge of the question

Let us assume that you are writing your final examination in a literature course, and the questions have not been set in advance. From a list of questions on John Steinbeck's novel *The Grapes of Wrath,* you select the following question: How do the various settings employed in *The Grapes of Wrath* illustrate how unrestrained capitalism undermines the essence of the American Dream? The question is worth fifty marks out of a total of 100 marks. Since the examination is two hours in length, you allow yourself one hour to plan and write the answer.

First, spend a few minutes brainstorming the question and jotting down relevant ideas and information to help you plan your response. Arrange your main points in a Basic Outline, and then create a Skeleton Outline containing the supporting details. As we demonstrated earlier in the manual, the outlines provide a formula for developing your paragraphs. In a shorter examination answer, the Basic Outline establishes the paragraph structure, while the Skeleton Outline supplies the supporting details. Once the structure is mapped out with the supporting details, it is a relatively easy task to write the essay. A sample response to the examination question is shown on the following pages. Since you already understand the outlining process, we have not provided outlines for the answer. As an exercise, you may wish to "deconstruct" the sample answer and create a Basic and a Skeleton Outline.

In The Grapes of Wrath, John Steinbeck employs a number of settings to show how unchecked capitalism undermines the essence of the American Dream. Whether it is the heartless bankers who evict the Joad family from their land at the beginning of the novel, or the ruthless fruit growers in California who exploit the Joad family at the end of the novel, it is capitalist greed that stands between the landless Joads and their dream of once again becoming self-reliant landowners. The Joads' dream of regaining their own plot of land – and with it their freedom, dignity and self-respect – is constantly frustrated by a system that rakes in profits at the expense of the individual.

The first setting in which we see the Joads is the family farm in Oklahoma, where the Joads for generations have been living out an agrarian version of the American Dream, a dream in which an individual farmer can work his own land free from interference. It is a time when the cumulative effects of years of poor land management and the recurring droughts of the Depression era are forcing people such as the Joads off their land. The family farm – the one institution that united and sustained rural communities – is being destroyed and taken over by banks and "owner men," concerned only about making a profit from the land. Their way of life destroyed, the Joads are forced to move farther west to California, a "promised land" where they hope to revive their dream.

After selling most of their possessions, the Joads load what they need into their jalopy and set off for California. The road is the next major setting. As life for the Joads unfolds on the road, a new social order develops, with different rules and codes of conduct than prevailed on their Oklahoma farm. It is a social order in which the sense of community is heightened by the collective suffering of the dispossessed at the hands of the harsh, profit-driven system that exploits them. Both their collective loss and their shared dreams for a brighter future in the West fill their lives on the road with a warm sense of comradeship.

The only labour available in California is fruit-picking, but it is controlled by ruthless proprietors who pay minimal wages and force workers and their families to stay in decrepit, unhygienic camps. In these camps, the Joads lose whatever sense of individualism they once possessed, and they despair of ever rediscovering the "dream." It is ironic that the one island of hope they discover in this sea of grime and poverty is a camp run by the government, a camp founded not on rugged individualism and self-reliance — values associated with the American Dream — but on communal cooperation. The setting of the camps suggests that the dispossessed cannot find self-respect in a world of exploitive capitalism, but only in a world where the worst excesses of capitalism are constrained either by custom or law.

Forced to leave this island of refuge to seek work, the Joads are once again thrust into the hostile world of capitalism. The final setting of the novel finds them in an abandoned railway boxcar in the midst of torrential rains and a sea of mud. In this bleak landscape the Joads struggle to survive: Tom Joad, the eldest son, is on the run from the police, and Rose of Sharon, the daughter, gives birth to a stillborn child after having been abandoned by her husband. The family is as broken as their dream of re-establishing themselves on their own land. The "dream" has been co-opted by the bankers and "owner men," leaving the Joads trapped in a nightmare of poverty and servitude, without dignity or self-respect.

Steinbeck places his characters in settings that show how unfettered capitalism makes a mockery of the ideals of individual freedom and self-reliance upon which America was supposedly founded. For it is the rapacious and unrestrained freedom of the "owner men" that reduces the Joads to a life of poverty and deprivation of freedom. Ironically, it is only by surrendering some individual freedom — in the communities on the road and in the government work camps where communal interests take precedence — that the Joads find some relief, and some little hope for a better life.

Comparisons

Comparative questions are frequently set in literature examinations. If you have practised the techniques of comparative analysis described earlier in this manual, you will not find comparative examination questions intimidating. Comparative questions can be open-ended, such as "Compare and/or contrast Richard III and Macbeth are tragic heroes" or more specific, such as "Contrast the characterizations of Biff and Happy in Arthur Miller's play *Death of a Salesman*." Some questions may be so specific that even the similarities and/or differences may be spelled out by the examiner.

Let us assume that the following question has been set on a final examination: Compare the ways in which the different narrative points of view affect the portraits of Hagar Shipley in *The Stone Angel* and Elinor Dashwood in *Sense and Sensibility*. The question is worth fifty marks out of a total of 100 marks. Since the examination is two and a half hours in length, you allow yourself an hour and a quarter to plan and write the answer. Remember that "compare" allows you to focus on either similarities or differences, or on a combination of both similarities and differences. In the earlier comparative essay, you were required to explain how the theme of light was explored by two poets, Emily Dickinson and William Wordsworth. You compiled a list of literary devices that directed your initial thinking, subsequent analysis, and final structuring of the essay. In this instance, the two devices that will direct your comparative analysis are spelled out in the question: narrative point of view and character (the "portraits" mentioned in the question).

Since the structure of a comparative essay is more complex than that of a single-focus essay, you must allow more planning time. **Do not start writing your answer until you have planned the structure.** Spend a few minutes reflecting on the question and brainstorming the main similarities and/or differences that explain how the narrative points of view control the manner in which the two major characters are portrayed. Jot these similarities and/or differences down on a piece of paper. You may not be able to cover all the similarities and/or differences in your response because of time constraints. Therefore, you may have to be selective when setting up your Basic Outline and focus on only the most important features. The next step is to structure the Skeleton Outline with the supporting details for each section. Since this is a comparison, you are not simply describing the two main characters. The two novels must be linked together with corresponding examples and details drawn from each work, to demonstrate how the two characters are portrayed by the use of narrative viewpoint.

Once the structure is mapped out with the supporting details, it is easy to weave your response together. The outlines will shape the paragraphs, as explained earlier in the manual. **Remember that comparisons are essays with a thesis or argument.** State the thesis concisely in the introduction and ensure that the sections of the body clearly demonstrate the connections and relationships stated in the thesis. Finally, complete your answer by drawing the links together and summing up the comparison in the conclusion.

Margaret Laurence's The Stone Angel *and Jane Austen's* Sense and Sensibility *are narrated from different points of view, and this significantly affects how the main character in each novel, Hagar Shipley and Elinor Dashwood, is portrayed. The specific point of view chosen by each author is calculated to accentuate certain characteristics of these principal characters, whose portraits are central to each novel's purpose.* The Stone Angel, *narrated from Hagar Shipley's point of view, presents us with a character who is proud and uncompromising. Hagar's stubbornness and paranoia, which we witness first hand, is intensely felt.* Sense and Sensibility, *told in the third person by an omniscient narrator, stresses Elinor's serenity and common sense. The narrator portrays Elinor from a more dispassionate distance, permitting us few glimpses of her inner turmoil, so that, by contrast, her composed and tranquil demeanour remains largely undisturbed.*

The different narrative viewpoints influence the portrayal of the state of mind of each character. Seeing events solely from Hagar's biased viewpoint, the reader is exposed to all of her misconceptions about herself and others. So strongly opinionated is she that we eventually come to recognize that her judgments, somewhat detached from reality, are unreliable. When, for example, Hagar is faced with the fact that she has been wetting her bed, she immediately denies it, despite its evident truth. Such denials are frequent throughout Hagar's life. By contrast, Elinor's reasonableness and sound judgment, hallmarks of her character, are accentuated because we do not share her every thought. The more detached third person narrator reports Elinor's words and actions, only rarely revealing her thoughts. By keeping Elinor at an emotional distance, we can more readily accept her as a calm, collected and stable character, and come to rely more on her interpretation of events.

Another effect of the different narrative viewpoints is that similar actions taken by Hagar and Elinor take on quite different meanings because of the way they are revealed. Hagar's biased narration forces the reader to interpret events from her point of view; therefore, the reader always needs to be wary of Hagar's accounts, whereas the question never arises with Elinor because we trust the omniscient narrator implicitly. For example, both Elinor and Hagar place great value on decorum, especially when displaying emotion. In <u>Sense and Sensibility</u>, the narrator describes Elinor's refusal to admit openly her feelings about Edward Ferrars as admirable and in keeping with the accepted conventions of the time. Elinor's apparent good judgment remains unchallenged by the reader because we are inclined to believe the narrator. However, Hagar's refusal to "hug" Marvin at the train station as he departs for war because she might be embarrassed by such a show of affection does not suggest good judgment, but rather a stunted ability to show love. Hagar's attempt to explain her action in the first person only intensifies our feelings of disgust for her stubbornness. On the other hand, Elinor benefits from *the approval of the detached narrator and acquires further dignity for suppressing her feelings.*

Finally, the narrative point of view affects our response to Hagar and Elinor by the way other characters are reported to perceive them. For example, Hagar Shipley leads us to believe throughout most of the novel that John, her younger and favourite son, returns her affection in equal measure. It is only at the end of the novel that we understand John's contempt for his mother, a contempt which Hagar may have sensed but never acknowledged because of her biased favouritism, and which was, therefore, concealed from the reader. Frequently the reader is left to piece together the opinions of other characters about Hagar, a task made more difficult because as the narrative unfolds it becomes increasingly clear that Hagar's views of others is distorted by her own blinkered perceptions. By contrast, it is clear from the outset of <u>Sense and Sensibility</u> that Colonel Brandon values Elinor's good sense. We never question this judgment by the omniscient narrator. Likewise, the kindly Mrs. Jennings thinks the world of Elinor, an opinion that reinforces our view of Elinor as serene and sensible. As we grow to distrust Hagar's account of how other characters view her, her stubborn pride and blindness to her own faults become more dramatically evident. Elinor's good sense remains in the foreground throughout the novel by the way other characters react to her.

Margaret Laurence and Jane Austen use different narrative viewpoints to achieve different effects. In <u>Sense and Sensibility</u>, the more distant and detached third person omniscient narrator allows Austen to paint a portrait of Elinor as a tranquil, serene woman whose feelings are carefully controlled and whose judgment is invariably sensible. Hagar Shipley's distorted perceptions and turbulent feelings are on display throughout the <u>The Stone Angel</u>. The narrative point of view chosen by Laurence allows her to accentuate the blindness, stubborn pride and lack of sound judgment that characterizes Hagar.

Commentaries

A commentary requires that you respond to a poem by explaining and supporting what you perceive to be its meaning. It is **your** interpretation of the poem that is required, not simply a line-by-line paraphrasing or summary of the poem. Your instructor is inviting a fresh interpretation — one arising out of your own personality and life experiences, not crafted from the thoughts and critical judgments of others.

Your first reading will prompt a response which may remain subconscious until you reread and analyze the poem. While rereading it, jot down those thoughts, insights, and feelings prompted by the poem that will help you articulate your perception of the meaning. This analytical process is similar to the method described earlier in the poetry comparison, although you will have to modify the process for an examination question because of time constraints. To assist you in your efforts to articulate your response, you should list the most significant poetic devices employed, such as imagery, symbolism, metaphor, setting, rhythm, and tone. Isolating the most relevant devices is an effective means of analyzing a poem, but it need not always control the design and substance of your comments.

Read the poem again, questioning and analyzing, and applying your creative imagination. After careful reflection and reference to your notes, you must decide how you are going to organize your comments to support your interpretation of the poem. **Although interpretations are subjective, they must be supported by reference to the text.** Just as with the other essays on literature, you must plan your commentary and illustrate it with relevant examples from the poem. Set up a Basic and a Skeleton Outline so that you can compose a coherent, comprehensible, and convincing commentary.

Let us assume that one of Margaret Atwood's poems, "Death of a Young Son by Drowning," has been included in a literature examination. You are required to provide your interpretation of the poem in a commentary of 800–1000 words. In the sample response that follows, you will notice that the commentary has an interpretation that is clearly expressed in the introduction and then developed and supported by a selection of quotations and ideas from the poem.

Death of a Young Son by Drowning

He, who navigated with success
the dangerous river of his own birth
once more set forth

on a voyage of discovery
into the land I floated on
but could not touch to claim.

His feet slid on the bank,
the currents took him;
he swirled with ice and trees in the swollen water

and plunged into distant regions,
his head a bathysphere;
through his eyes' thin glass bubbles

he looked out, reckless adventurer
on a landscape stranger than Uranus
we have all been to and some remember.

There was an accident; the air locked,
he was hung in the river like a heart.
They retrieved the swamped body,

cairns of my plans and future charts,
with poles and hooks
from among the nudging logs.

It was spring, the sun kept shining, the new grass
lept to solidity;
my hands glistened with details.

After the long trip I was tired of waves.
My foot hit rock. The dreamed sails
collapsed, ragged.

    I planted him in this country
    Like a flag.

Margaret Atwood

Basic Outline

A. Introduction

B. I. Mother's changing attitudes
   II. Impact of son's suffering on mother
   III. "Bathysphere" metaphor
   IV. Mother's epiphany and final acceptance

C. Conclusion

Skeleton Outline

A. Introduction

A mother, who has driven her son to live up to her expectations, recognizes that she has pushed him too far and finally accepts both his limitations and her unrealistic expectations.

B. I. Mother's changing attitudes
   - her love initially rests on her ambitions for her son
   - her love becomes more nurturing and tender

   II. Impact of son's suffering on mother
   - son forced into disaster
   - lack of son's strength to live up to mother's expectations
   - mother recognizes her ambitions for son are too great

III. "Bathysphere" metaphor
- son's perception is distorted by mother's ambitions
- son is unable to see clearly and save himself

IV. Mother's epiphany and final acceptance
- mother views son's body and recognizes his limitations
- realizes she has used him to fulfill her ambitions, not his
- she accepts things as they are

C. Conclusion

The poem depicts, through a mother's memory, the death of a child. This is not, however, a literal death, but rather the end of a phase of her son's life. It is an emotional death, for both him and his mother. The mother, who has strived to accomplish so many frustrated ambitions by living vicariously through her son, has pushed him into a way of life that he cannot handle. Driven by his mother, he does what is expected of him but finds that he cannot cope with her ambitions for him. His inadequacy, when it reveals itself, destroys the hope that his mother had initially vested in him; at the same time, she recognizes that she has erred.

The boy's precarious birth foreshadows the dangers that await him in life. While a firm bond is created between mother and son at birth, the mother's love for her son rests more on the possibilities that he represents for her than on his own qualities. It is only in the final stanza that there is exhibited the tenderness usually associated with mothers. "I planted him in this country/like a flag" represents the nurturing expected of a mother which she neglected to provide earlier in her son's life, after he had "navigated [. . .] the dangerous river of his own birth."

The mother, who at first attributes her son's survival at birth to him alone, finally realizes that she too has played a part in ensuring his well-being and her last action is one of a more expansive love.

Where the mother perceives that she has failed in her life, she expects her child to succeed, to valiantly venture "into the land I floated on/but could not touch to claim." Pushed by his mother, the boy's feet slide "on the bank" and he is forced into inevitable disaster. He soon discovers that he does not have the strength to conquer all that is desired by his mother. He is tossed and battered as "he swirled with ice and trees in the swollen river." As the boy "plunged into distant regions," he is thrust in over his head, yet fails to recognize his danger, captivated as he is by the "landscape stranger than Uranus." Never will he be able to withstand the current of the river, to live up to the vast and torrential expectations of his own mother. By placing all her hopes in him, she is slowly and unwittingly preparing the means of her son's demise. She almost suffocates her son with boundless demands, so that when her ambitions for him strangle him, he is "hung in the river like a heart" — her heart, engulfed by her disappointment. His predicament has an emotional impact on her that she has never realized before. Like her hopes, his body is battered and bruised.

At first, undaunted by the task before him because he is blinded by his youth as much as strengthened by it, he ventures where he should not go. Looking beyond the buffer, his "bathysphere," everything is distorted by his "eyes' thin glass bubbles." So the boy is made reckless by his youthful inexperience which shields him from the bitter truth that he cannot live up to his mother's aspirations. Instead, he sees only that which he has been taught to see, unwittingly deluded by his mother's ill-placed ambitions to the point of believing in the possibility that he can achieve them. From inside his shelter the son glimpses only a small, warped portion of the whole picture so that he never recognizes the passion which drives his mother and which is projected onto him.

Not principally concerned with the welfare or happiness of her son, the mother watches him struggle and then fail. His remains are pulled free from the tirelessly demanding grasp of the "nudging logs" efficiently and ruthlessly "with poles and hooks," not tenderly. She finally accepts that the "cairn of my plans and future charts" is unable to live the life she had plotted for him. After a lifetime of anticipation and uncertainty, she finally acknowledges her loss and, perhaps more importantly, her disappointment with her own life. She manages to live without the passionate ambitions for her son that have animated her life: "My foot hit rock. The dreamed sails/collapsed, ragged." Those feelings which drove her to drive her son relentlessly, dissipate as though they were only a part of a dream. Since she no longer regards her son as a means of fulfilling her dreams, her world ceases to be full of turbulent conflicts, and she can finally cherish the simple beauties of life and motherhood: "It was spring, the sun kept shining, the new grass/lept [sic] to solidity."

Life and contentment, both for the mother and her son, become possible once she has recognized the error of her ways. The last symbolic gesture she makes suggests that her son will have a chance to be free of her domineering influence. By planting him in "this country like a flag," she shows her pride in him and her acceptance of how he will make his own life-choices. Her final action is an anticipation of new beginnings.

The best craftsmanship always leaves holes and gaps in the works of the poem so that what is not in the poem can creep, crawl, flash, or thunder in.

Dylan Thomas

Glossary

Essay questions can be phrased in a variety of ways. Some questions may be specific, such as "Why do the women in T.S. Eliot's poetry ask so many unanswered questions?" Others may require a response to a quotation, such as "The aim of art is a heightened awareness of reality. Would you agree with this statement?" Comparative questions are especially common in examinations. Whether you are commenting on a poem, comparing two characters, or responding to a quotation, an examination answer requires that you develop and present an interpretation or point of view. You are not summarizing a short story, paraphrasing a plot, or describing a character. The keyword in each question will indicate the type of response required. Consult your instructor about ambiguous terminology, such as "analyze" and "discuss" before the examination. Listed below are some of the more common terms used in examinations.

Analyze: Identify and examine carefully the important details and ideas and explain their relationship and/or demonstrate their significance.

Analyze the images of death and mortality in W.H. Auden's poem "Lay your sleeping head, my love, . . ."

Comment: Explain or interpret a statement or quotation.

F. Scott Fitzgerald once remarked that American lives have no second acts. Comment on the fates of three of the characters in Fitzgerald's *The Great Gatsby* in light of this remark.

Compare: Show the connection or relationship between different ideas, characters, or works by focusing on the similarities and/or differences.

Compare MacLennan's treatment of Tallard and Yardley as exemplars of French and English Canadians in *Two Solitudes*.

Contrast: Show the connection or relationship between different ideas, characters, or works by focusing on the differences only.

Contrast the characterizations of Biff and Happy in Arthur Miller's play *Death of a Salesman*.

Sometimes both "compare" and "contrast" are used in a question.

Compare and/or contrast Richard III and Macbeth as tragic heroes.

Compare and contrast Richard III and Macbeth as tragic heroes.

Demonstrate: Explain clearly and illustrate with examples.

Demonstrate the Freudian egotism in T.S. Eliot's "The Waste Land."

Discuss: Examine an idea from all perspectives and present a response with supporting evidence.

Discuss Tennyson's reflections on death and memory in "In Memoriam."

Explain: Examine an idea and clarify its meaning.

Explain "soma" as it is used in Huxley's *Brave New World*.

Illustrate: Demonstrate with examples.

Illustrate Marlow's colonial mentality in Conrad's *Heart of Darkness*.

Interpret: Explain the meaning of an idea or a quotation.

Interpret Pope's statement: "A little learning is a dangerous thing; / Drink deep, or taste not the Pierian spring:"

Justify: Support and defend an argument or an interpretation with evidence and reasons.

Justify the claim of modern critics that Chaucer's Wife of Bath is a feminist figure.

Refute: Oppose an argument or an interpretation with evidence and reasons.

Refute the popular charge that Hamlet is not a tragic figure, but simply indecisive.

Significance: Demonstrate the importance of an idea in relation to the work as a whole.

What symbolic significance does the green light at the end of the Buchanan's dock have to the meaning of *The Great Gatsby*?

NOTES

1. Lucile V. Payne, *The Lively Art of Writing* (Chicago: Follett, 1965), 19.

2. Harry F. Wolcott, *Writing up Qualitative Research,* Qualitative Research Methods Series, vol. 20 (Newbury Park, CA: Sage Publications, 1990), 69.

3. Edward de Bono, *CORT 1: Teachers' Notes* (New York: Pergamon, 1973), 7.

4. R. J. Shafer, ed., *A Guide to Historical Method* (Homewood, IL: Dorsey Press, 1974),101.

5. Sheridan Baker, *The Practical Stylist,* 7th ed. (New York: Harper and Row, 1990), 43.

6. William Zinsser, *On Writing Well,* 6th ed. (New York: HarperCollins, 1998), 84.

7. William Strunk and E.B. White, *The Elements of Style,* 4th ed. (Boston: Allyn and Bacon, 2000), 72.

8. Sylvan Barnet and Reid Gilbert, *A Short Guide to Writing about Literature* (New York: Addison-Wesley, 1997), 300.

9. Gordon Taylor, *The Student's Writing Guide for the Arts and Social Sciences* (Melbourne: Cambridge UP, 1989), 160.

10. Rosalie Maggio, *The Non-Sexist Word Finder: A Dictionary of Gender-Free Usage* (Boston: Beacon, 1988), 170.

11. Joseph Gibaldi, ed., *MLA Handbook for Writers of Research Papers,* 5th ed. (New York: MLA, 1999), 33.

12. Payne, 61.

13. Zinsser, 17.

14. *ONLINE! FAQ* (12 January, 1998).<http://www.smpcollege.com/online-4styles~help/faq1.html> (1 December, 1999), chapter 1.

WORKS CONSULTED

Barnet, Sylvan and Reid Gilbert. *A Short Guide to Writing about Literature.* New York: Addison-Wesley, 1997.

The Chicago Manual of Style. 14th ed. Chicago: University of Chicago Press, 1993.

Fabb, Nigel and Alan Durant. *How to Write Essays, Dissertations, and Theses in Literary Studies.* London: Longman, 1993.

Gibaldi, Joseph, ed. *MLA Handbook for Writers of Research Papers.* 5th ed. New York: MLA, 1999.

Harnack, Andrew and Eugene Kleppinger. *Online! A Reference Guide to Using Internet Sources.* New York: St. Martin's Press, 1998.

Maggio, Rosalie. *The Non-Sexist Word Finder: A Dictionary of Gender-Free Usage.* Boston: Beacon, 1988.

Mann, Thomas. *The Oxford Guide to Library Research.* New York: Oxford University Press, 1998.

Payne, Lucile V. *The Lively Art of Writing.* Chicago: Follett, 1965.

Pirie, David B. *How to Write Critical Essays: A Guide for Students of Literature.* London: Methuen, 1985.

Roberts, Edgar V. *Writing about Literature.* 9th ed. Upper Saddle River, NJ: Prentice Hall, 1999.

Strunk, William and E.B. White. *The Elements of Style.* 4th ed. Boston: Allyn and Bacon, 2000.

Taylor, Gordon. *The Student's Writing Guide for the Arts and Social Sciences.* Melbourne: Cambridge University Press, 1989.

Turabian, Kate L. *A Manual for Writers of Term Papers, Theses, and Dissertations.* 6th ed. Chicago: University of Chicago Press, 1996.

Zinsser, William. *On Writing Well.* 6th ed. New York: HarperCollins, 1998.

INDEX

"Death of a Young Son by Drowning" from *Selected Poems 1966-
1984* by Margaret Atwood. Copyright © Margaret Atwood 1990.
Reprinted by permission of Oxford University Press Canada.

"A Light Exists in Spring" by Emily Dickinson is reprinted by permission of the Estate of Robert N. Linscott, Editor.